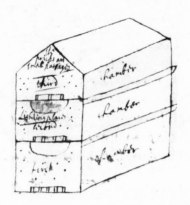

third

chamber

Lighting place
brood

chamber

first

chamber

TOLSTOY
TOGETHER

ALSO BY YIYUN LI

TOLSTOY TOGETHER

85 DAYS OF
WAR AND PEACE
WITH
YIYUN LI

EDITED BY BRIGID HUGHES

A PUBLIC SPACE BOOKS

A PUBLIC SPACE BOOKS
PO BOX B
NEW YORK, NY 10159

A Public Space gratefully acknowledges the generous
support of the Drue and H. J. Heinz II Charitable
Trust, the Chisholm Foundation, the New York
State Council on the Arts, the Amazon Literary
Partnership, and the corporations, foundations, and
individuals whose contributions have helped to make
this book possible.

 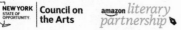

LIBRARY OF CONGRESS CONTROL NUMBER: 2020946090
ISBN: 978-1-7345907-6-0
EISBN: 978-1-7345907-7-7
DISTRIBUTED BY PUBLISHERS GROUP WEST (PGW)

DESIGN BY DEB WOOD
WWW.APUBLICSPACE.ORG

9 8 7 6 5 4 3 2 1

That is its greatest beauty. In some mysterious way, the reader collaborates with the text and brings it to life. The art of writing depends on the art of reading.

MICHAEL SILVERBLATT

TABLE OF CONTENTS

INTRODUCTION

ONCE UPON A TIME, five people with strong opinions were invited to view an old tree and offer their thoughts.

The first one says: "I'm a big-picture person. At first glance, I can say this tree is too big for its own good. We need to lop some limbs off."

The second one says: "It's not the architecture of the tree that bothers me but the parts that make up the whole. Anywhere I direct my attention, I can see ten or twenty imperfect leaves."

The third one says: "This tree is much too old to be relevant. Its life began when the world was wrong in many ways: patriarchal, despotic, undemocratic. Why should we care about something growing out of that history?"

The fourth one says: "The world is still wrong in many ways. A tree like this does little to solve the political, socioeconomic, and environmental issues of today."

The fifth one says: "I am not a tree person. Roses and nightingales are worthy subjects of my attention, and I consider it an insult to my talent to be asked to look at a tree."

Anytime one talks about *War and Peace*, one is reminded of the tree's critics. Fortunately, a majestic tree has no need for a defender.

—

Our literary litmus paper is made, at least partially, by the impressions and memories of our senses. If a book were full of details never seen, heard, smelled, tasted, or felt by us, we might be more mystified than a goose or a cockapoo would feel when confronted with our literature, which to them must be outlandishly vague. Yet greedy readers—I count myself as one—crave more than a confirmation of experience: we want writers to articulate that for which we haven't yet found our own words, we want our senses to be made uncommon.

Books that I feel drawn to and reread, *War and Peace* among them, are full of uncommon sense and common nonsense. (Uncommon nonsense makes exhilarating literature, too, in Lewis Carroll's case, but uncommon nonsense does better to stay uncommon: in less skillful hands, it becomes caprice or parody.)

One imagines that Tolstoy did not seek to write about uncommon sense. He simply presented the world, and the world, looked at closely, is often extraordinary. A line I never tire of in *War and Peace*:

> The transparent sounds of hooves rang out on the planks
> of the bridge.

Colors are regularly described as "muted" or "loud," but sounds that are transparent make a reader pause. The ringing hooves take me back to my early childhood in Beijing, where cars were scarce, and flatbed horse trailers passed in the street, carrying coal, lumber, produce, and sometimes people huddled together. Forty years later, I can still hear those horses walking down the narrow path outside our apartment on winter mornings as I lay awake, the sky dark but for a thin patch of paleness in the east, a predawn color called *yu du bai* (fish-belly white) in Mandarin. And there—when the outdoor and indoor were visible with shapes but not colors, when the tip of my nose turned cold if I let my head surface from the burrow between the quilt and the pillow (the heating in the building was only turned on from 7:00 P.M. to midnight), when, contrary to reality yet common to children's perception, the world was still new and I was old enough for everything—there went the tapping of the hooves, clippity-clop, clippi-ty-clop, a sound like no other, metallic, clear, yet without any harsh or sharp edge. Transparent—yes, and tangible.

"One who sees so much and so well does not need to invent; one who observes imaginatively does not need creative imagination," Stefan Zweig said of Tolstoy. One who sees so much and observes imaginatively also makes the best demand of his readers: to read unhurriedly as one must live unhurriedly, with imagination, which is akin to reverie.

—

Although moments of uncommon sense abound in *War and Peace*, they are no more than the grace notes in the novel. Tolstoy's interests were in humans and their limitations, in nations and their histories. Readers, whether they are reading during the Stalingrad battles (Vasily Grossman), or in a cramped high-school dorm in Beijing in the 1980s (a friend of mine), or, as during our first Tolstoy Together group, at the beginning of a pandemic (three thousand readers from around the globe, many under lockdown), must have no difficulty finding their worlds reflected in *War and Peace*: the man-made and natural catastrophes; the egomanias and incapacities in those designers of national and international schemes; the boundless human indifference; the inevitable human kindness; deceptions and strivings in marriages and in families; friendships and loves lost and found. The most absurd element of human absurdity, ironically, is that the absurdity is one of the most universal features—it would be a truly strange world if our absurdities turned out to be rare and unique. What binds people to one another more sturdily than our common nonsense? Even the Greek gods would have been forgotten had they been sensible.

> Anna Mikhailovna was already embracing her and weeping.
> The countess was also weeping. They wept because they were
> friends; and because they were kind; and because they, who
> had been friends since childhood, were concerned with such
> a mean subject—money; and because their youth was gone.

Tears in literature do not necessarily move the readers as they move their shedders. If I am asked to name five unforgettable scenes in all the books I have read that involve a character's tears, I may be able to offer only one example: the passage featuring Anna Mikhailovna and Countess Rostova is one of the moments in *War and Peace* I often reread. Their tears touch me because they are secondary characters in a book with over five hundred characters; because neither of them is quite sympathetic—they can be called selfish, snobbish, calculating, manipulative, vain, and they do not hesitate to mistreat and abuse people of lesser power or status; because they are mothers, and they interfere with their children's lives in the name of love; because life cares little about their love for their children—Anna Mikhailovna, widowed, has nothing to rely on to advance her son's career but her cunning, and Countess Rostova's many children have been taken by death too soon; because they are lifelong friends; because their friendship, destined to be lifelong, is cut short not by one or the other's death but by their pride, pettiness, and vindictiveness, by injuries caused by minor conflicts, by what is not in their control—the mean subject of money, the cruelty of war, the inadequate solace of peace.

And their tears stay with me because they are presented as who they are, with none of their traits amplified into an identity and their persons restructured around their identities. They are limited and yet expansive, superficial and yet complex, flawed and yet—at this one moment, when they embrace each other and weep, when the best qualities in one friend meet the best in the other—perfect.

—

What about common sense? Common sense in history, in philosophy, in religion, in the collective endeavor of human beings—isn't that what Tolstoy tried so hard to instill in his words? And yet I like to think that common sense is something I achieve for myself, after wading through uncommon sense and common nonsense. And I have not found a better book for that purpose than *War and Peace*. I don't imagine myself into any one of the characters, but I measure myself beside the characters: my conceit and aspiration against Andrei's, my clumsiness and bafflement against Pierre's, my youthful zeal and shame against Nikolai's, my blind willfulness against Natasha's, my sorrow against many mothers' sorrows, my daydreaming against Mlle Bourienne's. Fallibility is shared by all the characters; Tolstoy himself, too, was fallible. And that, I imagine, is the common sense I have come to for myself, through reading *War and Peace*, through living and remembering: fallibility is the only reliable factor in my life; fallibility is in everything I do.

Common sense—common to whom, you may ask. Not to those critics of the magnificent tree, certainly, but luckily, this is not a book for them.

YIYUN LI

When Tolstoy is telling a tale, we do not hear his breathing. He tells it as upland peasants climb their native hills; slowly, equably, step by step, without rushes, without impatience, without fatigue, without weakness; and the throbbing of his heart never troubles the smooth tone of his voice. That is why we do not lose our composure when we are in his company. Dostoeff-sky hurries us up to the dizzy altitudes of delight; suddenly plunges us into unfathomable abysses of misery; and then makes us soar with him in the dreamland of fantasy. But with Tolstoy we are wide awake.

STEFAN ZWEIG

AN IMPRECISE GUIDE
FOR TOLSTOY TOGETHER

You are holding in your hands an invitation. Turn the page and you arrive. There are all these faces, maybe you find yourself in a room full of strangers. You recognize no one. Or if you do, maybe you have been one of the thousands of people, across six continents, who participated in Tolstoy Together.

Let go, abandon yourself and absorb the rhythm. The cacophony of voices. Be part of the chatter in the different corners of the room.

This book is based on an experiment. At the start of the pandemic, a series of conversations with friends at A Public Space led to the idea of reading a novel together. Because a long novel seemed what the moment called for, *War and Peace* was decided on. We had been displaced from our usual world, and an immersion in a world elsewhere offered comfort. Almost like those who feel like a stranger in their homeland, and travel to a new land to be authentically a stranger.

We were to read slowly, but consistently—a half an hour each day. Every day. A Public Space would share a few observations from Yiyun Li on social media. Others would add their thoughts. On March 18, 2020, we started the novel and on June 10, 2020, eighty-five days later, we read our last pages.

This book is a road map of how to read an epic that many of us want to read but never quite find a way into. There are conversations about favorite characters, craft lessons elucidated, Tolstoy's philosophy and concealed structure, and most of all a way to read and see for future readings.

The reading schedule appears at the top of each day's chapter. The sections and passages where to start and end each day, are from the Richard Pevear and Larissa Volokhonsky translation, which is the edition used by Yiyun Li. Others read translations by Anthony Briggs, Ann Dunnigan, Rosemary Edmonds, Constance Garnett, Louise and Aylmer Maude. Some read translations in French, German, Japanese, Korean, Spanish. Some read the novel in Russian. Sometimes we got things wrong. We also disagreed.

You will figure out the rest.

And if you don't figure it out, just come along for the trip.

BRIGID HUGHES

Dear Friends,

Let's go—slowly,
without rushes,
without impatience,
without fatigue,
without weakness.
With some random
thoughts from me
and many more
from you.

YIYUN LI

DAY 1
MARCH 18

START
Volume I,
Part One, I
"'Eh bien, mon
prince'"

END
Volume I,
Part One, III
"the company
of intelligent
women."

YIYUN LI

How to begin a novel with hundreds of characters? As one manages a party with hundreds of guests.

As the owner of a spinning mill, having put his workers in their places, strolls about the establishment, watching out for an idle spindle or the odd one squealing much too loudly, and hastens to go and slow it down or start it up at the proper speed—so Anna Pavlovna strolled about her drawing room.

The skills of a successful soiree hostess: I once told a friend I learned how to host a party from the opening of *War and Peace*.

—

As a good maître d'hôtel presents, as something supernaturally excellent, a piece of beef one would not want to eat if one saw it in the dirty kitchen, so that evening Anna Pavlovna served up to her guests first the viscount.

Anna Pavlovna, the hostess, presents the viscount to her guests as a piece of beef. From a dirty kitchen!

—

"Charmant," said Anna Pavlovna, looking questioningly at the little princess. "Charmant," whispered the little princess, sticking the needle into her work as if to signify that the interest and charm of the story kept her from going on working.

Anna Pavlovna needs the little princess's support for even the most cliché reply; and the little princess needs an extra prop for her performance. (Even the best actors lose their confidence!)

—

All the guests performed the ritual of greeting the totally unknown, totally uninteresting and unnecessary aunt.

The poor aunt—doesn't she remind us of Freddy Malins's mother in James Joyce's "The Dead," placed at "a remote corner." In every party there is an unnecessary and inconvenient guest.

A FOUNDING EPIC

So many of the opening scenes of *War and Peace* take place in drawing rooms, where manners and propriety and gossip rule, and war seems very far away. One senses, from the beginning, the way the social order will be destabilized. **ELLIOTT HOLT**

If asked to predict how the novel would open, I, a fool who had never so much as cracked the spine, would have said panoramic sweep—not gossip at such beautiful close range. **DAN CHIASSON**

This is why I love Tolstoy. It's the close–up psychological precision and commentary on society that always brings me back. **ELLIOTT HOLT**

For Russia, *War and Peace* has always been a founding epic. Tolstoy once said to Maxim Gorky, Without false modesty, it is like the *Iliad*. In these early scenes, we see adopted French culture on full display. By the end, Russia will have found itself. **JOHN NEELEMAN**

Remembering that Tolstoy was a big fan of *Walden*, a book that is more about systems and communities (and how to rewire yourself to improve them) than its public reception would indicate. **ROBERT SULLIVAN**

"I love a broad margin to my life." **HENRY DAVID THOREAU**

"'Can one be well while suffering morally? Can one be calm in times like these if one has any feeling?' said Anna Pávlovna."
Already staggered by the cast of characters, my usual response to Tolstoy, but she's the one I'd most like to join for tea. So far. **WAYNE SCOTT**

Tolstoy moral judge already. Grateful, universal, empathic, quietly outraged. **DIANE MEHTA**

"'I often think,' she continued after a short pause, drawing nearer to the prince and smiling amiably at him as if to show that political and social topics were ended and the time had come for intimate conversation—'I often think how unfairly sometimes the joys of life are distributed.'"
The first thing that strikes me is how much humor there is in *War and*

Peace, right from the start. I completely missed it the first time around. To be fair to younger me, that was in high school, when much of life's comedy went zipping over my head. **DENY FEAR**

High points so far: Prince Vassily's casual, if not amused, acceptance of being a terrible father (this is very autobiographical for Tolstoy, no?). And the description of Pierre, from Anna Pavlovna's perspective, as *"the young man who did not know how to live."* **MATT BURNS**

> My translation (Edmonds) gives the line about Pierre a slightly different emphasis: the *"young man who did not know how to behave."* **ROBERT BUTLER**

> Yes but it's so great when it's "live"—because I have so often felt like that. How did everyone else get the rules on how to live but I somehow did not? **CARMEN ZILLES**

"As is always the case with a thoroughly attractive woman, her defect— the shortness of her upper lip and her half-open mouth—seemed to be her own special and peculiar form of beauty."
This passage about Princess Bolkonskaya's upper lip has been running through my head since I first read it in high school, and deeply colored my view of female beauty; it's nice to remember these small, personal moments. It's the first time I remember encountering (in literature, at least) the idea that human beings are more beautiful in their imperfections, and I love it very much. **ADRIENNE CELT**

Writers all have writerly tics, descriptions and parts of the bodies that we return to again and again (flushed faces, beating hearts, you know what I mean). For Tolstoy, perhaps it's lips and mouths? **S. KIRK WALSH**

Tolstoy is the great cataloguer of nineteenth-century Russian lips. Are writers missing the boat when they lavish so much attention on eyes? **BOB HILLMAN**

Smart choice by the translators (Pevear and Volokhonsky) to leave the French untranslated in the text—the close scrutiny required to "listen" (either by translating it yourself or using the notes) puts the reader right in that room. DAN CHIASSON

> Disagree! I'm glad I can move through without interruption because the French has been translated for me within the text. CARL PHILLIPS

> Navigating between the two languages is going to end up being like watching the two armies move in and out of each other in fog, through hills and valleys, pursuing each other, extending each other, interrupting each other. The book is in many ways also about these two languages and their histories. JORIE GRAHAM

I did not realize that Tolstoy had written *Anna Karenina* *after* *War and Peace*, and I must admit that it makes me glad—I'm rereading *Anna Karenina* right now and it was such an education for me as a writer in psychological acuity; I'm excited to be reading *War and Peace* for the first time. ESMÉ WEIJUN WANG

> Man, you're in for a total treat! *War and Peace* is much sillier at times than *Anna Karenina*, but such fun! Like, a real delight. If *Anna Karenina*'s a lemon tart of some kind, *War and Peace* is pure cake! COLIN WINNETTE

> LOL. I love the idea of Tolstoy books as different kinds of baked goods. ESMÉ WEIJUN WANG

Vasily Grossman at the Battle of Stalingrad: "Grossman's daughter, Yekaterina Korotkova, concludes a brief summary of her volume of memoirs with the words: 'I remember a letter of his from Stalingrad: Bombers. Shelling. Hellish thunder. It's impossible to read.' And then, unexpectedly: 'It's impossible to read anything except *War and Peace*.'" PHIL KLAY

I woke up early this morning and sank into Tolstoy. Never read *War and Peace* before and a sense of calm descended. *"Soyez tranquille, Lise."* MEGAN CUMMINS

DAY 2
MARCH 19

START
Volume I,
Part One, IV
"Anna Pavlovna
smiled"

END
Volume I,
Part One, VI
"'Word of
honor!'"

YIYUN LI

A first encounter with a character in Tolstoy is an encounter with the character's essence.

He did not, as they say, know how to enter a salon, and still less did he know how to leave one.
     Pierre reminds me of Winnie the Pooh, and is as dear to me.

—

Two footmen, one the princess's, the other his, waiting for them to finish talking, stood with shawl and redingote and listened to their French talk, which they could not understand, with such faces as if they understood what was being said but did not want to show it.

Even the minor characters in *War and Peace* are never boring. Tolstoy's footmen remind me of Rebecca West's butler in her novel *This Real Night*:

> Now the butler, who had maintained his character
> as a Shakespearean courtier by moving a couple
> paces away from us with an air of withdrawing
> to another part of the forest, came forward and
> opened a door at a blank verse pace.

—

I never quite understand why Prince Andrei married Lise. Though I have a feeling he would be sympathetic toward Kierkegaard's view of marriage:

> Take a young man, ardent as an Arabian horse,
> let him marry, he is lost. First of all the woman is
> proud, then she is weak, then she faints, then he
> faints, then the whole family faints.

SERIALITY AS A STATE OF MIND

Such a pleasure to start anew, and keep to fifteen pages a day. Recapturing a bit of the rhythm and sense of anticipation of Tolstoy's original readers awaiting the next installment of "The Year 1805" (*War and Peace*'s original title) in the periodical the *Russian Messenger*. EILEEN CHENG-YIN CHOW

> Tolstoy's original readers knew what was in store for these characters and their way of life. Now we're the characters *and* the readers. How will our world change? MISS MAINWARING

> The footmen—they're us. We're marginal but central. We know so much these souls don't know. Tolstoy's party scene is the perfect lesson in how to regard our own POV as readers. DAN CHIASSON

Seriality as a state of mind, a habit of body, a particular way of knowing the world. Seriality connoting linearity. Serially reading *War and Peace*, serially following these stories' trajectories to a happy ending—or so we hope. EILEEN CHENG-YIN CHOW

Is anyone rereading *War and Peace*, or revisiting? I read it mostly in a busy corner cafe in Brussels, servers bustling, scooping up tips, spilling Belgian beer. The context is different now and will require tuning out a different sort of noise. Where were you? SARAH BLAKLEY-CARTWRIGHT

I found a pair of old photos of myself in high school in my copy of *War and Peace*. I love discovering little histories in old books. ADRIENNE CELT

> Reading my grandfather's copy of *Anna Karenina*, after he died, I found a piece of paper with a diagram of all the characters, their nicknames, and relationships to each other; he'd used it as a bookmark. How lovely to think about books being part of other lives—earlier generations, or our younger selves. PAULINE HOLDSWORTH

Tolstoy spent 1863 to 1869 writing and rewriting *War and Peace*. In those five years, his new bride, Sophia, gave birth to four children, while copying and editing the full manuscript seven separate times. A different kind of serial rhythm. EILEEN CHENG-YIN CHOW

I'm struck by Tolstoy's ability to bring a number of characters together in one scene and then move on. Gather and disperse. Gather and disperse. All the while so many relationships are being set up. **S. KIRK WALSH**

Tolstoy fills the novel with eyes—everyone is watching—using their glances to depict character: Hélène's egoistic examination of her body; the count's withering glance at his wife. Anna Pavlovna's constant watching for the wrong social moves of her guests. **PHILIP F. CLARK**

Incredibly detailed and intimate descriptions of faces. Charles Baxter said we don't describe faces enough in our current literature. Just a few pages into *War and Peace* and I am reminded how right he is. **AYANA MATHIS**

> I've been working on this for two weeks (a description of a face)—extremely hard, and psychological, making it even more difficult to do right. **DIANE MEHTA**

> Tolstoy is brilliant on faces. (In this pre-photographic era, people would not have seen "natural" images of themselves, capturing their features unawares. At most, they would have seen a portrait, or their own self-conscious image in a mirror.) **MICHAEL G. FAULKNER**

> I swear it's not just the days of self-isolation that have made me obsessed with Tolstoy's descriptions of human faces. **PIA DESHPANDE**

I'm enjoying the way Tolstoy describes the cast as a crew of so-so actors. Prince Vassily *"spoke lazily, the way an actor speaks a role in an old play."* Meanwhile, Pierre seems to be operating on another plane, feeling people for who they are and making them feel, feel specifically in a way that is at odds with their role—at a party, in society, in relationships. Pierre makes people feel uncomfortable. He is like a truth serum, a disrupter. **ROBERT SULLIVAN**

"There's nothing more important for a young man than the company of intelligent women." Amen, Vasily. **MISS MAINWARING**

"She evidently forgot her age and employed, out of habit, all her old feminine resources."
A brutal portrayal of older women. **ANNE MCGRATH**

So far I've learned that Princess Hélène has lovely shoulders, and that no one will mind if you're socially awkward if you adopt a *"kindly, simple, and modest expression."* **ANSA KHAN**

Has anyone ever noticed that Tolstoy's women are either young and beautiful or old and wrinkled? From what I can tell, the bewitching age is forty. I will try not to hold this against him as I read. **HEATHER WOLF**

Also love how Tolstoy's first descriptor for all male characters is height. Sizing them up. **ALEXANDRA SCHWARTZ**

A query for Russian historians: what was the assumed "normal" stature for a man in this era? Tolstoy seems inordinately fixated—every man is introduced thus: *"of medium height," "unusually tall," "not very tall."* **EILEEN CHENG-YIN CHOW**

The Standard of Living and Revolutions in Russia, 1700–1917 by Boris Nikolaevich Mironov gives the average height of military recruits in the Napoleonic period at ~161 cm (or 5'3"). **ERIK M. GREGERSEN**

Not quite an answer to your question: At Yasnaya Polyana, Tolstoy's bed was smaller than my son's single bed; his desk and chair were minute. He was 5'11" but the chair, very low, didn't look comfortable enough for anyone over 5'2". **YIYUN LI**

My favorite thing about Tolstoy's Moscow house (preserved as a museum) are the little barbells near his desk. When I went to visit the museum, I loved imagining him doing an arm workout during writing breaks.[1] **ELLIOTT HOLT**

1 Joshua Rothman from the *New Yorker* remembered that in *Anna Karenina*, Levin was annoyed and frustrated so he did something with his barbells and then all was right again.

DAY 3
MARCH 20

START
Volume I,
Part One, VI
"It was already
past one
o'clock"

END
Volume I,
Part One, X
"she slowly
walked beside
him to the
sitting room."

YIYUN LI

I often discuss Tolstoy with my masseuse, who was born in the Ukraine. Once, I asked her where the bear in the carousing scene came from. She said they must've stolen the bear from a circus.

I said, Oh, I didn't think of that.

"What did you think? That bears walk around in Moscow, and they grabbed one off the street?"

I thought people would go bear hunting.

"In that case, you'd only get a dead bear."

—

Countess Rostova had twelve children, but only four are alive when the novel opens. Tolstoy only mentions this once (but the lost ones are ever present in what she does).

—

The sound of several men's and women's feet running to the door, the crash of a tripped-over and fallen chair, and a thir-teen-year-old girl ran in.

Tolstoy slyly puts a veil over the omniscience so we are the guests now, not knowing... and waiting to meet... Natasha.

THE START OF A JOURNEY

This is my first time reading *War and Peace*. So far I'm seeing characters' weaknesses, small-mindedness, pettiness, vacuousness... all very elegantly and beautifully done, but also... cruel? CLAIRE ADAM

But aren't we all like this? I love his wry take on humanity. It'll make any good act or small change so much more significant. MICHELE SMART

He makes them seem so small and stupid, is what I mean. From where is the enjoyment to be derived? CLAIRE ADAM

These characters are at the start of a journey. Some become more noble, some less so, in response to the coming crisis. All become more *themselves*. It's more like real life than any other novel I've ever read. MARGARET HARRIS

"But at once, as happens with so-called characterless people.... the thought occurred to him that the word he had given meant nothing, because before giving his word to Prince Andrei, he had also given Prince Anatole his word... finally he thought that all these words of honor were mere conventions with no definite meaning, especially if you considered that you might die the next day, or something so extraordinary might happen to you that there would no longer be either honor or dishonor."

(The trouble is, you never die the next day.) ALEXANDRA SCHWARTZ

Characterless. The one word stunned me. PHYLLIS COHEN

Pierre is profoundly easy to love, but I have always had such a disaster-crush on Dolokhov. Hard to defend when his intro is chugging a bottle of rum while dangling out a window, but there it is. OLIVIA WOLFGANG-SMITH

How many people have been at a party where someone is doing something ridiculously dangerous and yet you don't want to interrupt and be the party pooper—alas, I would've been the one hiding in the washroom as Dolokhov risked death. Then I would've peeked out after about forty-five minutes: "Is he dead yet?" ESMÉ WEIJUN WANG

AWKWARD BUT NOT EMBARRASSED
YIYUN LI

Pierre asked awkwardly, as usual, but without embarrassment.

One distinctive trait of Tolstoy's writing is his repetition (a tendency that today would be discouraged by teachers and editors). In the scene with Boris and Pierre, it's the repetition of the words *"awkward"* and *"embarrassed."* (I hadn't notice it until a friend pointed it out. So much for paying attention; we often need another pair of eyes to understand what fascinates us.)

Awkward but not embarrassed: What kind of people are this way? I've always loved Pierre, but couldn't articulate my love until I saw the distinction Tolstoy makes between these adjectives.

Awkwardness indicates a kind of lacking—physical skills or social skills—that is visible to the world. Pierre is awkward in many ways. He makes people uncomfortable, but these are people who act according to a shared script—and those who do not err from the script have a singular advantage over those who do.

Embarrassment, to me, refers to an entirely different kind of self-consciousness. It is about what remains invisible to the world but visible to oneself. If I'm humming a song to myself—I am not a good singer—I'm neither embarrassed nor awkward. If another person overhears me, I may feel awkward because my singing isn't good enough for others' ears. But I wouldn't feel embarrassed—after all, I'm not a professional singer, and I accept my limits. I would, however, feel embarrassed if I read some of my published work and see a line that is not good enough. Perhaps no reader would recognize that. And yet, such a line would remain an embarrassment.

Pierre is always trying to find a place for himself in the world, and in that struggle he bumbles and is full of awkwardness. But he knows exactly who he is, what he wants from life—he only does not know how to get it. All his pursuits in the novel—religion, numerology, carousals, reformations, marriage, love. All of these pursuits will place him in different kinds of awkwardness, but he doesn't feel embarrassed by any one of them. He is doing his best to be who he wants to be—there is never embarrassment in that. YIYUN LI

TOLSTOY'S INTRODUCTIONS

What a treat to realize the title *War and Peace* actually refers to the complicated mother-daughter relationship between Countess Rostov and her *"least favored"* daughter. The way the countess dismisses Vera (*"Can't you feel that you're not needed here?"*) is so savage, and also really makes me miss my mom.

PS: I want to learn how to *"smile disdainfully."* NICK WHITE

Rereading a novel you love is always a special gift to yourself. For all the time I have spent reading and rereading this book, the remarkable exchange between Boris and Pierre had not stuck with me. Now it will never cease to make me glad. JOHN NEELEMAN

How delightful to take time over revisiting beloved and despised characters. Watching how Tolstoy introduces them at first, hinting at who they really are. Looking at you, young Boris. KELLY GARDINER

"And Boris, with an evident sense of having discharged an onerous duty, having extricated himself from an awkward position, and put somebody else into one became perfectly pleasant again."

Tolstoy reminding me why I've been social distancing for forty years. CARL PHILLIPS

Boris: One of the best war strategists in peace time. YIYUN LI

It's easy to judge Boris. But in eighteenth-century Russia, there weren't many avenues to social or economic advancement for the son of a poor single mother. There are less appealing ways to success than by charm. JOHN NEELEMAN

I'd like Boris to be my companion. Not only is he *"young, trim, and handsome,"* he also explains who everyone is: *"'You are mistaken,' Boris said unhurriedly, with a bold and slightly mocking smile. 'I am Boris, the son of Princess Anna Mikhailovna Drubetskoy. The Rostov father is called Ilya, the son is Nikolai.'"* ROBERT DEAM TOBIN

Don't sleep on Boris, he will take your mama's pension and leave you with a smile. ANNIE LIONTAS

YIYUN LI

START
Volume I,
Part One, XV
"Countess Rostov,
with her
daughters"

END
Volume I,
Part One, XVII
"letting out a
long, deep
breath and
pushing up
her sleeves."

The most agreeable occupation... was the position of listener, especially when he managed to set two garrulous interlocutors on each other.

I very much share Rostov's preference: winding up two jumping frogs is better than being wound up and made to jump.

—

His conversation was always concerned with himself alone; he always kept calmly silent when the talk was about something that had no direct relation to himself. And he could be silent like that for several hours.... But as soon as the conversation concerned him personally, he began to speak expansively and with obvious pleasure... as though it was obvious to him that his success would always constitute the chief goal of everyone else's desires.

Berg cheers me up: I hope (?) I haven't reached a point for Tolstoy to lance me with his words.

—

The German tutor tried to memorize all the kinds of dishes, desserts, and wines, in order to describe everything in detail in his letter to his family in Germany, and was quite offended that the butler with the napkin-wrapped bottle bypassed him. The German frowned, trying to show by his look that he did not even wish to have this wine, but was offended because no one wanted to understand that the wine was necessary for him, not in order to quench his thirst, nor out of greed, but out of a conscientious love of knowledge.

The prototype of an Instagrammer? Still, I love that the paragraph ends with *"love of knowledge."* And I shiver at how Tolstoy makes a character transparent.

THE WEIGHT OF THE PRESENT MOMENT

Was there any laughter at Anna Pavlovna's soiree in Saint Petersburg (besides Ippolit's idiotic laughter at his own incomprehensible joke)? In Moscow, the Rostov house is positively ringing with laughter. **THOMAS J. KITSON**

I don't know what I expected of *War and Peace*, but it wasn't a bunch of drunk dudes carousing Moscow with a bear. **BARBARA VANDENBURGH**

> Ah, but the carousing happened in Petersburg! Moscow is the unfashionable, backward Asiatic place you get exiled to after you make posh, sophisticated European Saint Petersburg too hot to hold you—the contrast between the cities is an ongoing theme. **MARGARET HARRIS**

The best part about these domestic scenes is that we're able to witness what a good time you can have by staying inside. **JEFFERY GLEAVES**

"He was an inconvenience and was the only one not to notice it." One of my greatest fears. **RUBY WANG**

"Why do you keep banging on the table?" she asked the colonel. "What's all the noise about? You haven't got the French here you know."
"I speak ze truce," came the smiling reply.
"It's war talk," the count shouted across the table. "My son's going, Marya Dmitriyevna. He's off soon."
"I have four sons in the army, but I don't go on about it. We're all in God's hands."

I remember a debate one holiday in my family about US policies of isolationism versus involvement... my uncle is the German colonel. **TAYLOR MICHAEL**

Reading these so-familiar remarks about world affairs in a setting so far-flung from our own is the very power of art, and has lowered my blood pressure immediately. **ADRIENNE CELT**

The endpaper of my 1942 edition of *War and Peace* shows the presence of both Napoleon and Hitler in Russia. The weight of the present moment on the fiction of the past. **LAURA SPENCE-ASH**

DAY 6
MARCH 23

START
Volume I,
Part One, XVIII
"Just as the
sixth *anglaise*
was being
danced"

END
Volume I,
Part One, XX
"Pierre went out."

YIYUN LI

The death of old Count Bezhukhov leads to the first real war in the novel. Bloodless battles are often fought more heartlessly than bloody ones. One feels internally wounded just by reading.

The vultures gather, and the story kicks into gear. What better way to pass an hour in an otherwise empty laundry room? **RON HOGAN**

"The princess had the air of someone who has suddenly become disappointed in the whole human race." Same, girl. Same. **KIMBERLY BURNS**

The undertakers circling the house—Tolstoy's characters never behave well around the deathbed (cf. *Ivan Ilyich*, which follows two decades later, and people are still rude). **WAYNE SCOTT**

—

He went over to him, took his hand... and pulled it down, as if testing whether it was well attached.

Prince Vassily's hands speak more eloquently than his words.

I love Tolstoy's attention to awkward logistics: *"In his right hand, which lay palm down, a wax candle had been placed between the thumb and the index finger, held in place by an old servant who reached from behind the armchair."* **LAURA PRESTON**

—

Waiting for his father's death, twice Pierre is described with both hands on his knees, *"in the naïve pose of an Egyptian statue."*

LESSONS FOR ACTORS

The next act. Tolstoy the director positions everyone in relation to the deathbed—the actors in their poses, and us in relation to them. Richard Maxwell's *Theater for Beginners* has my favorite acting lessons. **FRANNIE**

> **YOU ARE THE ACTOR.** Your body brings in something, call it presence, and it happens by degrees. Arms, chest, haunches and thighs, calves and feet. The body, firing synapses, in between and in the gray matter. On and off. The billions of cells, the body mechanisms, the busy regulating, the adjusting, the retinas contracting and expanding, body secreting, beating, moving, breathing and pulsing. Your being registers here. Swallow. Inhale. Open mouth to press air out to touch the flesh in the throat to make sound.

> **YOU ARE THE ACTOR.** A thing of flesh and feeling. Perfect because you aren't. You find atmospheric peace where time disappears. You prolong the inevitable. You carry forward. Your progress, your excellent-ness, your victory gets identified and claimed by us. We take it. Your self-destructive pleasures, your secrets, vices, shame and guilt, individual and universal; we take that too. We know your desire and all its peculiar shape. You play different characters in the eternal.

> **I AM THE AUDIENCE MEMBER.** I sit down and there is a void between us. I can't stay with you in time. I race ahead, or I lag behind. As I watch, the moment is already disappearing. I am yearning for moments as they occur, predicting moments that haven't. How can we manage this, to be in the past, present and future, in the same room, watching the same play?...

> —

> **YOU ARE THE ACTOR AND I AM THE AUDIENCE MEMBER.** We face the gap from either side. You open your mouth to speak—!!—to reach out over the chasm, and I will meet you. And the divisions will cease to matter. **RICHARD MAXWELL**

DAY 7
MARCH 24

YIYUN LI

START
Volume I,
Part One, XXI
"There was no
one in the
reception
room now"

END
Volume I,
Part One, XXIII
"'Go to the
dining room.'"

Having talked with Pierre, Anna Mikhailovna drove off to the Rostovs'... and told the Rostovs and all her acquaintances the details of Count Bezukhov's death. She said that the count had died as she would like to die, that his end had been not only touching, but also instructive; and the last meeting of the father and son had been so touching that she could not recall it without tears, and that she did not know who had behaved better in those terrible moments: the father, who remembered everything and everyone so well in the last minutes and said such touching things to the son; or Pierre, who was a pity to see.

The only match for Anna Mikhailovna is Prince Vassily. Such a pity he didn't court her, but courted her best friend (Countess Rostova) instead. If only these two were a couple—what wouldn't they have snatched from the world?

—

"Well, aren't you a fool!" shouted the prince, shoving the notebook away, but he got up at once, paced about, touched the princess's hair with his hands.

Princess Marya is old Prince Bolkonsky's fool, just as Cordelia is King Lear's fool.

—

Julia Karagin's letter saves us from having to read ten more chapters on how old Count Bezukhov's will gets sorted out. A good gossip is a good assistant to a novelist.

OUR FELLOW READERS

"If the world could write by itself, it would write like Tolstoy." ISAAC BABEL

"His method is one of deliberate slowness and contemplation, a contemplative slowness that brings order and unity out of confusion." SAUL BELLOW

"After one has read *War and Peace* for a bit, great chords begin to sound.... They come from the immense area of Russia, over which episodes and characters have been scattered, from the sum-total of bridges and frozen rivers, forests, roads, gardens, fields, which accumulate grandeur and sonority after we have passed them.... Space is the lord of *War and Peace,* not time." E. M. FORSTER

"We feel that we know his characters both by the way they choke and snooze and by the way they feel about love and immortality and the most subtle questions of conduct." VIRGINIA WOOLF

"I have felt everywhere—in a sense—you will know what I mean—that sublime indifference to the life or death, success or failure, of the chief characters, which is not a blank indifference at all, but almost like submission to the will of God." C. S. LEWIS

"Tolstoy's life has been devoted to replacing the method of violence for removing tyranny or securing reform by the method of non-resistance to evil. He would meet hatred expressed in violence by love expressed in self-suffering. He admits of no exception to whittle down this great and divine law of love. He applies it to all the problems that trouble mankind. GANDHI

"It is awkward to differ from a great man, but Tolstoy was wrong. Kings are not the slaves of history. History is the slave of kings." TONI MORRISON

"Despite the heaps of evidence that Tolstoy was in reality half crackers, you would swear from the pages of *War and Peace* that he was God's stenographer." CLIVE JAMES

"I'd like somebody to write a book that really told the truth about life now. Leo Tolstoy but with drive-through windows." NICHOLSON BAKER

DAY 8
MARCH 25

START
Volume I,
Part One, XXIV
"At the appointed
hour"

END
Volume I,
Part One, XXV
"shook his head
reproachfully,
and slammed
the door."

YIYUN LI

"Well, now, Mikhail Ivanovich, things are going badly for our friend Bonaparte. Prince Andrei... has just been telling me what forces are being prepared against him! But you and I always considered him an empty man."

Mikhail Ivanovich, who had no idea when this you and I had spoken such words about Bonaparte, but who understood that he was needed in order to launch into the favorite subject.

Every talker stands on the shoulders of a *"wordless"* character.

—

Old Prince *"flung away his plate, which was deftly caught by Tikhon."*
Some characters need two hundred pages to come alive. Tikhon needs only one line.

—

She and Mikhail Ivanovich are the two persons with whom he's always gentle and kind, because he's their benefactor. As Sterne says: "We love people not so much for the good they've done for us, as for the good we've done them."

One place I've raised my eyebrow: Laurence Sterne was one of Tolstoy's favorite authors (he even translated him). But is Princess Marya the kind of character who would like his work? She mostly reads religious books.

THE SORROW OF PARTING

"Nobody's going to get me in any ring with Mr. Tolstoy unless I'm crazy or I keep getting better": It's easy to see why Hemingway admired Tolstoy during the pages of Prince Andrei's departure from the Bolkonsky estate—a masterclass of the "iceberg theory." **MATT GALLAGHER**

Prince Bolkonsky and Marya—what a pair. One forgets Tolstoy's sense of humor was a dry and wonderful thing. **FIONA MAAZEL**

"From the study, like gunshots, came the oft-repeated angry sounds of the old man blowing his nose."
Hearing rather than seeing the old prince in distress at his son leaving for war. A lovely way to access his sorrow. **LAURA SPENCE-ASH**

Very struck by how Tolstoy depicts the old prince's fear and sadness at seeing his son go off to war. Sometimes humorous (throwing the plate), sometimes heartbreaking. **LAWRENCE COATES**

"From her big eyes shone rays of a kindly and timid light. These eyes lit up her whole thin, sickly face and made it beautiful.... Andrei understood, made the sign of the cross, and kissed the icon. His face was at the same time tender (he was touched) and mocking."

A beautiful scene at the Bolkonsky estate, when Marya gives her brother Andrei the icon. And then the leave-taking. Tolstoy takes no sides, gives Marya's beliefs a true hearing. Already the fox who longed to be a hedgehog (per the great Isaiah Berlin essay on Tolstoy). **MURRAY SILVERSTEIN**

Tolstoy's mother was named Marya Nikolaevna Volkonskaya, just one letter off from Princess Marya Nikolaevna Bolkonskaya I think there's so much tenderness in the writing of this character, who seems in some ways to be a loving recreation of his mother. **MOLLY ELIZABETH PORTER**

Names always matter in fiction. Pierre Bezukhov means Peter the Earless: he can't hear, he's tone-deaf. When I learned that Dr. Zhivago means Dr. Living (not Dr. Life but the ongoing present), it changed that whole story for me. **CATHERINE OATES**

DAY 9
MARCH 26

YIYUN LI

START
Volume I,
Part Two, I
"In October 1805"

END
Volume I,
Part Two, III
"But the cornet
turned and left
the corridor."

When people say you can skip the war parts of *War and Peace* and read the peace parts only, they may be saying: Let's pretend we could skip this pandemic (or any catastrophe, uncertainty, inconvenience) and make the world go as we want it to.

—

He turned away and winced, as if wishing to express thereby that all that Dolokhov had said to him and all that he could say had long, long been known to him, that it all bored him, and that it was all by no means what was needed.

Just as battles played out in the drawing rooms, the battlegrounds turn into drawing rooms. Kutuzov knows more than anyone that the army is just another soiree, and everyone is expected to stay predictable.

—

You are looking at the unfortunate Mack.

Tolstoy suspends his narrative omniscience when he wants a character's entrance to be dramatic. Mack shows up as Natasha did, causing a gasp somewhere.

THE REGIMENT STIRRED

When I was young, I skipped the war parts, to follow the adventures of the young people. Well, I skipped the military-history parts. Now I find them the most fascinating, and Kutuzov as the very heart of the novel. **KELLY GARDINER**

Tolstoy has a simile that Homer would be proud of (I imagine): *"The regiment stirred itself like a bird settling its feathers, then all was still and silent."* Fusing military and nature is how so many similes work in the *Iliad*. **CARL PHILLIPS**

Zherkov, a minor comic character worthy of Shakespeare. Dolokhov, the mysterious upstart and Pierre's buddy. An attire change so that *"the square had been transformed from black to gray."* Tolstoy brings a regiment inspection to life as only he can. **MIKE PALINDROME**

"We're either officers, who serve their Tsar and their country and rejoice in the success, and grieve at the defeat of the common cause, or we're hirelings, who have no interest in our master's business."
Prince Andrei at the top of his game. **DEWAINE FARRIA**

"Sir, if you insist on acting like a buffoon," *he began cuttingly, with a slight trembling of the jaw,* "it is not for me to stop you, but if you *dare play the fool once more in my presence I'll teach you how to behave."*
Andrei calling Zherkov a clown, as war approaches, reminds me of Henry IV's rejection of Falstaff. **ANNIE LIONTAS**

My King, my Jove, I speak to thee, my heart. **FALSTAFF**

I know thee not, old man. Fall to thy prayers.
How ill white hairs become a fool and jester.
I have long dreamt of such a kind of man,
So surfeit-swelled, so old, and so profane;
But being awaked, I do despise my dream. **HENRY IV**

Tolstoy begins to tighten the screws on naive frivolity! **SIGRID PAUEN**

And to move us from a romantic view of war to reality. **ELLIOTT HOLT**

DAY 10
MARCH 27

START
Volume I,
Part Two, IV
"The Pavlogradsky
hussar regiment"

END
Volume I,
Part Two, VII
"'Put a stick
between your
legs, that'll do
you for a horse,'
rejoined the
hussar."

YIYUN LI

Through marches, reviews, battles, retreats, tableaux of historical figures and their fictional subordinates, Tolstoy never lets out of his sight Prince Andrei and Nikolai Rostov, who carry the chronology of the war between them.

—

The Russian officers' approval of their infantrymen ransacking a village in Austria, their jokes about violating the nuns: civilians' fates are treated with light, almost jesting touches—until the French army enters Russia.

—

At the bend of the Danube one could see boats and an island, and a castle with a park, surrounded by the waters of the Enns falling into the Danube; one could see the left bank of the Danube, rocky and covered with pine forest, with a mysterious distance of green treetops and blueish gorges. One could see the towers of a convent looming up from the pine forest with its wild and untouched look, and far away on a hilltop, on the other side of the Enns, one could see the mounted patrols of the enemy.

There must be a word in German to describe this effect? From the legato of the scenery to the arresting note of the mounted patrols of the enemy, already within sight.

TOLSTOY IS TO DOSTOEVSKY
AS TCHAIKOVSKY IS TO RACHMANINOFF

Tchaikovsky is the paterfamilias of Russian classical music. His symphonies, concerti, and operas set the standard for all Russian composers. In Tchaikovsky, we hear structure, solidity, stateliness, elegance, clarity, and intense beauty.

How can we not think of Tolstoy, Tchaikovsky's contemporary and compatriot? He too gives us structure, solidity, stateliness, elegance, clarity, and intense beauty. The structure of the novel's four volumes, with distinct subparts and chapters? A great Tchaikovsky symphony, almost all of them in four movements, each with subsections and themes. The clarity of Andrei's battle-induced vision of a *"distant, lofty, and eternal sky"*? The reflective second theme of the first movement of the Pathétique (about four minutes in). The tender beauty of Pierre's feelings for Natasha under a streaking comet? The gorgeous French horn theme in the slow movement of Tchaikovsky's Fifth.

Tchaikovsky fused Russian musical themes with classical European art forms dating to Mozart and Beethoven. In *War and Peace,* we have European (French) language, a French-loving Russian aristocracy, even for a period a Russian protagonist's admiration for Napoleon himself.

In Tolstoy's characters, we almost hear the distinct melodies of Tchaikovsky's twelve Seasons. The unrestrained, exuberant purity of Natasha (April as a young woman, January at the end). The quiet, inner tragedy of Princess Marya (March). The sadness of Andrei, only rarely feeling the joy and wonder of love and life (June). The carefree, dancing Count Rostov (July). The roguish gambler Dolokhov (August). The innocent youth of Sonya (December). And Pierre, always searching, questioning, and discovering, while living the sweep of history (November). Imagine if these melodies in the Seasons could speak to one another, befriend one another, fall in and out of love with one another? Tolstoy lets us imagine.

Rachmaninoff, like Dostoevsky, is another matter. Rachmaninoff is more passionate, obsessive, ruminating. The last movement of his Third Piano Concerto, its relentless, almost insane drive, recalls Porfiry's pursuit of Raskolnikov in *Crime and Punishment.* Rachmaninoff, like Dostoevsky, is also the darker of the great masters, murkier, more brooding, more "Russian."

When Natasha visits her uncle, she abandons herself to the joys of dance, music, and the Russian spirit. In the worlds of these four geniuses, we can only do the same. ILANN M. MAAZEL

"And Tushin went over to the general, putting three fingers to his visor in a timid and awkward movement, not as military men salute, but as priests bless."

My favorite moment in all of Part Two, though I can't say why, is this. I mean obviously Tushin is the best, but this gesture is absolutely heartbreaking to me, and I wish I could explain it to myself.

GARTH GREENWELL

DAY 11
MARCH 28

YIYUN LI

START
Volume I,
Part Two, VIII
"The rest of
the infantry"

END
Volume I,
Part Two, IX
"a long-past,
far-off memory."

He looked at the squadron that was moving toward him. The transparent sounds of hooves rang out on the planks of the bridge as if several horses were galloping, and the squadron, with officers in front, four men abreast, stretched across the bridge and began to come out on the other side.

Colors are sometimes "muted" or "loud," but we don't often see *"transparent"* used to describe sounds.

—

Rostov, sent with his colleagues to set fire to the bridge, could not help *"because, unlike the other soldiers, he had not brought a plait of straw with him."*
    One has to have a soft spot for a boy so bravely playing in a man's game.

—

"Two hussars wounded and one killed on the spot,*" he said with obvious joy, unable to hold back a happy smile, sonorously rapping out the beautiful phrase* killed on the spot.

The first death in the war, giving the colonel a chance to love his own words.

WAR LITERATURE

War literature is much more ranging and literary than a lot of smart book folk often allow. But if the "genre" needed to be pared to one line: *"And the fear of death and of the stretchers, and love of the sun and of life, all merged into one feeling of sickening agitation."* **MATT GALLAGHER**

"They shoot not because they want to but out of expectation."
    I'm surprised (like so many of us) by how absurdly the war is depicted. Not many heroes. Several people have compared it to *Catch-22* but something about this line brings Tim O'Brien to mind. **RICHARD Z. SANTOS**

What did people think about Nikolai's epiphany on the bridge: *"How good the sky seemed, how blue, calm and deep..."* I couldn't repress the feeling that Tolstoy was making fun of his dreamy idealism. **ROBERT DEAM TOBIN**

Just before the first battle: *"A particular brilliance and joyful sharpness of impression to everything that happens in those moments."* Then, after the first time under fire: *"It's all over, but I'm a coward, yes, I'm a coward, thought Rostov."* **MURRAY SILVERSTEIN**

Something that amazes me in *War and Peace* is the range of affect in the narration—from the very moving tenderness with which it treats Rostov under fire (*"but I'm a coward, yes, I'm a coward"*) to the brutal objectivity of the panoramic summary that starts the next chapter. **GARTH GREENWELL**

    Also did anyone else gasp to learn that *"the sick and the wounded had been left on the other side of the Danube with a letter from Kutuzov entrusting them to the humaneness of the enemy,"* or was it just me? **GARTH GREENWELL**

Tolstoy really knows how to capture scorn. **FIONA MAAZEL**

I'm enjoying the descriptions of the unconvincing expressions people adopt when speaking to others. **ANSA KHAN**

Today I learned Nabokov read *War and Peace* at age eleven. **RYAN CHAPMAN**

DAY 12
MARCH 29

YIYUN LI

START
Volume I,
Part Two, X
"Prince Andrei
stayed in Brünn"

END
Volume I,
Part Two, XIII
"women of
their mutual
acquaintance."

His thin, drawn, yellowish face was all covered with deep wrinkles, which always looked as neatly and thoroughly washed as one's fingertips after a bath.

I don't understand Tolstoy today. Bilibin is thirty-five and lives comfortably. Who loans him this face?

—

Prince Ippolit needs only one gesture. His *"examining his raised feet through his lorgnette"* is as immortal an image as when he *"stood beside the pretty, pregnant princess and looked at her directly and intently through his lorgnette."*

—

On the roadsides one constantly saw now dead horses, skinned or unskinned.

Anyone can write the horror of a dead horse in war; Tolstoy makes a dead horse deader.

BILIBIN'S FOREHEAD

With Rostov we saw war up close, as ordinary soldiers see it. With Prince Andrei we saw it as the generals see it. And now, with Bilibin, we see it as a diplomat sees it. The three views are completely different—and all are masterfully described. **MARGARET HARRIS**

His words *"were of a transmissible nature, as if designed to be easily remembered and carried from drawing room to drawing room by insignificant society people."* Bilibin invents the meme. **ANNIE LIONTAS**

Bilibin's Twitter game would have been strong. **KIRTAN NAUTIYAL**

I'm imagining Bilibin as a Russian version of Oscar Wilde—the sort of chap who plans his off-the-cuff remarks well in advance, just in case they're needed. **MARGARET HARRIS**

"In society he constantly waited for the opportunity to say something remarkable... Bilibin's conversation was constantly sprinkled with wittily original and well-turned phrases of general interest."
And yet, I waited in vain for Bilibin to start spouting some of these gems. What a brilliant move on Tolstoy's part, to be born before "show, don't tell!" **ALIX CHRISTIE**

I'm so amused at the welcome Andrei receives by Bilibin's circle as *"one of ours,"* knowing he went to war to escape high society. **MICHELLE EINDHOVEN**

I'm listening to an audio version from England, and all the nobility speak with plummy, posh accents, like Boris Johnson, while the soldiers all sound like cockneys, or like they are from the Midlands. **LAWRENCE COATES**

The deep creases and wrinkles on Bilibin's face speak a language of their own—he allows the creases to run off his forehead *"in token of being done with the subject."* **ZULMA ORTIZ-FUENTES**

Who does he look like? I can't see it. **TERESA FINN**

Bilibin's forehead is my favorite new character. **ASH MARTIN**

DAY 13
MARCH 30

START
Volume I,
Part Two, XIV
"On the first of
November"

END
Volume I,
Part Two, XVIII
"after the
disordered
French."

YIYUN LI

They talked of peace, but did not believe in its possibility. They talked of battle and also did not believe in the nearness of battle.

Perhaps when we say we live in history, it means we live in shared disbeliefs rather than individual ones.

—

"Prince Andrei smiled involuntarily" in the presence of Captain Tushin. Some people inspire awe. Others, jealousy. The best ones are those who make us behave unlike ourselves.

—

Marching into confrontation with the French, *"a company commander... was obviously thinking of nothing at that moment but the fine figure he would cut as he marched past his superior. With a parade-like self-satisfaction, he marched lightly on his muscular legs, as if floating, holding himself straight without the least effort... It seemed that all the forces of his soul were aimed at marching past his superior in the best possible way.... The soldiers curved around something at the spot where the cannonball had landed, and a decorated old soldier, a sergeant on the flank, after lingering by the dead men, caught up with his line, skipped to change feet, fell into step, and looked back angrily."*

When Tolstoy writes about the war, he is not only writing about the cannonballs and the bodies, but how people act despite the cannonballs and the bodies—both sensibly and near illogically.

A READING LIST

Tolstoy prepared for his publisher in 1891 a list of the works that had made an impression on him at each phase of life.

CHILDHOOD TO THE AGE OF 14 OR SO

The story of Joseph from the Bible. Tales from the *Thousand and One Nights*: The 40 Thieves, Prince Qamr-al-Zaman. *The Little Black Hen* by Pogorelsky. Russian byliny: Dobrynya Nikilich, Ilya Muromets, Alyosha Popovich. Folk Tales. Pushkin's Poems ("Napoleon").

AGE 14 TO 20

Matthew's Gospel: Sermon on the Mount. Laurence Sterne, *Sentimental Journey*. Rousseau, *Confessions; Emile; Nouvelle Héloise*. Pushkin, *Yevgeny Onegin*. Schiller, *Die Räuber*. Gogol, *Overcoat; The Two Ivans; Nevsky Prospect*; the story "Viy;" *Dead Souls*. Turgenev, *A Sportsman's Sketches*. Druzhinin, *Polinka Sachs*. Grigorivich, *The Hapless Anton*. Charles Dickens, *David Copperfield*. Lermontov, *A Hero of Our Time*; *Taman*. Prescott, *History of the Conquest of Mexico*.

AGE 20 TO 25

Goethe, *Hermann und Dorothea*. Victor Hugo, *Notre Dame de Paris*. Tyutchev's poems. Koltsov's poems. The *Odyssey* and the *Iliad* (read in Russian). Fet's poems. Plato's *Phaedo* and *Symposium* (in Cousin's translation).

AGE 35 TO 50

The *Odyssey* and the *Iliad* (in Greek). The byliny. Xenophon's *Anabasis*. Victor Hugo, *Les Misérables*. Mrs. Henry Wood's novels. George Eliot's novels. Trollope's novels.

AGE 50 TO 63

All the Gospels in Greek. Book of Genesis (in Hebrew). Henry George, *Progress and Poverty*. Theodore Parker, discourse on religious subject. Frederick William Robertson's sermons. Feuerback, *The Essence of Christianity*. Pascal's *Pensées*. Epictetus. Confucius and Mencius. Lalitavistara Sūtra. Lao-Tzu (S. Julien, French translator).

YIYUN LI

START
Volume I,
Part Two, XIX
"The attack o
the sixth
chasseurs"

END
Volume I,
Part Two, XXI
"Bagration's
detachment
joined Kutuzov's
army."

"Who are they? Why are they running? Can it be they're running to me? Can it be? And why? To kill me? Me, whom everybody loves so?"... The first Frenchman with the hooked nose came so close that the expression on his face could already be seen. And the flushed alien physiognomy of this man who, with lowered bayonet, holding his breath, was running lightly towards him, frightened Rostov. He seized his pistol and, instead of firing it, threw it at the Frenchman, and ran for the bushes as fast as he could... Quickly leaping over the hedges, with that swiftness with which he had run playing tag, he flew across the field.

Nikolai running as if playing tag: anyone can write about the loss of innocence in a war; Tolstoy writes about the return to innocence.

—

Tushin in action: *"He pictured himself as of enormous size, a mighty man, flinging cannonballs at the French with both hands."*
     The difference between a man with an ego and a man without one: Prince Andrei's superhero fantasy is joyless; Tushin's, gleeful.

—

He opened his eyes and looked up. The black canopy of the night hung three feet above the light from the coals. A dust of falling snow flew through that light.

The first snow in the novel: as atmospheric as Tchaikovsky's Symphony no. 1 (*Winter Dreams*); not yet the *1812 Overture*.

ALL THIS WAS SO STRANGE

One of my soldier's lives in Iraq was saved from a fire due to the quick thinking of the troop's "dirtbag"—the guy who wouldn't listen, was always pissing hot for drugs, etc. He and an interpreter cut open sandbags when the extinguishers weren't enough. Thought of this again while encountering Dolokhov's heroism at the front—so often the best combat soldiers don't look the part, they're not fit for parade, have the hardest time with regular life. Tolstoy knew his soldier types. **MATT GALLAGHER**

Two kinds of disappointment: For Prince Andrei, *"All this was so strange, so unlike what he had hoped."* For Nikolai Rostov, *"No one needs me... There's no one to help or take pity on me."* **THOMAS J. KITSON**

The Rostov scenes in today's reading... especially beautiful even for Tolstoy, even as they're just totally heartbreaking: *"Now it was not, as before, an invisible river flowing in the darkness, but like a gloomy sea subsiding and quivering after a storm."* **EMMA KIESLING**

I feel that Tolstoy has still spared us a lot. Dreamy, naive, narcissistic Nikolai Rostov (*"Me, whom everybody loves so?"*) is still alive. Lovable cooky Tushin with the bad shoes survives the battle and its aftermath, thanks to Prince Andrei. The dead are mainly anonymous, whisked by on stretchers, or left behind in the fields. **ROBERT DEAM TOBIN**

"Tushin came on behind riding his gunner's nag; he had lost all control of his emotions and said nothing to them, afraid to open his mouth because every word brought him inexplicably to the brink of tears."
   War is terrible. **JAYDON FARAO**

Such a wonderfully strange way for Tushin to separate himself from the battle at hand: *"In his imagination, the enemy's cannons were not cannons but pipes, from which an invisible smoker released an occasional puff of smoke."* **LAURA SPENCE-ASH**

"What, is a man to die like a dog." Not if the French army surgeon Dr. Jean Larrey could help it. Inventing triage and "flying" ambulances, he modernized field medicine under Napoleon. **SIGRID PAUEN**

I'm trying to catch up....
Don't want to retreat. Need
encouragement. Can you
help?

JOANNE HAYHURST

You can catch up! If you stop
now, you'll miss complete
changes of fortune, multiple
flung plates, a duel, dancing
with princesses, birth, tragic
deaths, people back from
the dead, cannonballs, war,
existential crisis, clouds on an
acid trip, more Pierre.

BRIAN OLSON

"Why is Tolstoy not coming?… Are you sure the bears really have not eaten him?" Turgenev wrote to a friend, when Tolstoy had not returned on time from a bear-hunting trip.

Friends who are worrying about catching up: Tolstoy was late, running behind schedule. We can be too, while reading War and Peace. As long as nobody is eaten by the bears, we shall prevail.

YIYUN LI

DAY 15
APRIL 1

START
Volume I,
Part Three, I
"Prince Vassily
did not think
out his plans."

END
Volume I,
Part Three, II
"the counts
Bezukhov in
Petersburg."

YIYUN LI

Pierre being duped into marriage reminds me of Horton being duped into hatching the egg:

> "ME on your egg? Why, that doesn't make sense."

> "Just sit on it softly. You're gentle and kind. Come, be a good fellow. I know you won't mind."

—

Especially the youngest, the pretty one with the little mole, who often confused Pierre with her smiles and her own confusion on seeing him.

A near love story crowded out by the army of society people enlisted into capturing Pierre for Hélène.

—

Prince Vassily's family is... complicated. His wife *"was tormented by envy of her daughter's happiness."* Hélène's brother *"Anatole was in love with her and she with him, and there was a whole story."*
    No wonder Ippolit needs a lorgnette—so much drama.

IT IS TOO LATE NOW, IT'S DONE

"In the excited state of a commander on the battlefield, when thousands of brilliant new thoughts come along one scarcely has time to bring to fulfillment—Anna Pavlovna, seeing Pierre, touched his sleeve with her finger." War invades the peace. **MICHAEL KELLEHER**

The war scenes slowly kill me, society brings me back to life. **CATHRINE LØDØEN**

The amorality of the matchmaking scheming is astonishing. Perfectly reflects Jane Austen: "It is a truth universally acknowledged..." **PHILIP MCGARRY**

The parallels between Pierre and Tushin. Both are quiet intellectuals with a need to please others and a fear of letting them down. Both are shunned and ridiculed. Pierre's disorientation at Hélène's party mirrors Tushin's in the final fight. Both men are placed in the midst of compromising situations (Pierre's expected proposal, Tushin's report to the general), and "congratulated" by ambitious men (Vassily, Andrei). They're left hopelessly confused. **AURELIA DRAKE**

Struck and delighted by three different perspectives of Pierre on one page: *"handsome and healthy"* by the guests (now that he's rich); *"red, fat, happy, and uneasy"* by the footmen; *"his unattractive face,"* Pierre of himself. **LAUREN GOLDENBERG**

What a difference time makes. Thirty years ago I was excited for Pierre that he captured this beauty. Today, it felt like he was being led to the slaughter. **PAUL SERVINI**

"'It is too late now, it's done; besides, I love her,' thought Pierre."
    Pierre's refusal to take agency of his own life is a bit vexing but also a refreshing contrast to the battle chapters where brash men pretend to be able to control all the disorder and ruin. **MATT GALLAGHER**

Read today's chapters with a knot in my stomach. Hoped until the end that Pierre would wake up and take control of his life from the cunning battleground commanders, Anna Pavlovna and Prince Vassily. What a defeat! **ZULMA ORTIZ-FUENTES**

DAY 16
APRIL 2

START
Volume I,
Part Three, III
"Old Prince
Nikolai Andreich
Bolkonsky
received
a letter"

END
Volume I,
Part Three, IV
"And, raising
her finger and
smiling, she
left the room."

YIYUN LI

A better husband than Prince Andrei *"would seem hard to find these days."* Old Prince Bolkonsky's parental blind spot is an occasion to try out a word I've never used: LOL.

—

Our regiment is already on the march. But I'm enlisted—what am I enlisted in, Papa?

Prince Vassily at least has a more clear-eyed assessment of his son— *"no genius, but he's an honest, good lad."*

—

Mlle Bourienne had a story, heard from her aunt, completed by herself, which she liked to tell over in her imagination... Now he, this real Russian prince, had come. He will carry her off, then ma pauvre mère *will appear.*

Mlle Bourienne, not the most heartbreaking woman, breaks my heart with her imagination—rather than a fantasy for romance, it's an orphan's dream of a reunion with her mother.

INVISIBLE LINES

Tolstoy is all about the empty spaces and invisible lines that we fear but are somehow compelled to cross—lines between two armies, between men and women, between life and death. BENJAMIN T. MILLER

"His plate did not seem clean to him; he pointed to a spot and flung it aside. Tikhon caught it and handed it to the butler."
    For those keeping score, a second plate tossed and caught. Tikhon clearly has this down. LAURA SPENCE-ASH

Brilliant, hilarious mirrors: just as the regiment must put back on its grubby greatcoats at the opening of part two, old Prince Bolkonsky forces his servants to unsweep the road so the despicable Kuragins travel *"over the road purposely laden with snow."* ALIX CHRISTIE

Right after a nine-year-old is described as speaking *"like an elderly brigadier,"* Tolstoy shows how childish adults can be. Wonderful subtlety, as befits mastery. CARL PHILLIPS

I all of a sudden like Old Prince Bolkonsky because he dislikes Vassily.
RICHARD L. GORELICK

The contrast between Anatole, effortlessly achieving *"scented foppishness"* without once looking in a mirror, prior to meeting Princess Marya, who Tolstoy has repeatedly and unhappily seeing herself in mirrors—his non-reflection, her painful *Oh!* CHARLIE SMITH

Now we're talking: *"Anatole's gaze, though directed at [Marya], referred not to her but to the movements of Mlle Bourienne's little foot, which he touched just then with his own foot under the pianoforte."* MURRAY SILVERSTEIN

Being able to see Anatole playing footsie with Mlle Bourienne while Marya imagines life with him—split screen. PATRICIA CLARK

"Could the joy of love, of earthly love for a man, be for her?... God gave her the answer in her own heart. 'Desire nothing for thyself, seek nothing, be not anxious or envious'... Princess Marya sighed."

DAY 17
APRIL 3

START
Volume I,
Part Three, V
"They all
dispersed"

END
Volume I,
Part Three, VII
"this hateful
little adjutant."

YIYUN LI

Anatole is predictable, but one has to love him when, caught with Mlle Bourienne, he *"with a merry smile, bowed to Princess Marya, as if inviting her to laugh at this odd incident."*
A cliché embodying its cliché-ness full-heartedly.

—

The hero Nikolai was once *"that son who had first learned to say 'brush' and then 'mama'"*—a detail only a mother does not forget, and a detail Tolstoy always remembers to include.

(PS: Is this how to say *"brush"* in Russian: *"shchetka"*? Harder than *"mama."*)

> Nikolai's first words in the Russian are груша (grusha) and баба (baba), which seem more like *pear* and *granny* to me (also to Garnett). **MOLLY ELIZABETH PORTER**

> I can't forgive Pevear and Volokhonsky for translating Nikolai's first word, *pear,* as *brush.* **ANNE RUNNING SOVIK**

—

Rostov, humiliated by Prince Andrei and fantasizing about aiming a pistol at his face, *"was surprised to feel that, of all the people he knew, there was no one he so wished to have for a friend as this hateful little adjutant."* Touché!

A JANE AUSTEN DAY

It was certainly a Jane Austen day for me. Between the prince advising Marya about Anatole's proposal and her freedom to choose (à la Mr. Bennet) and Marya's *Emma*-like promise to make a match between Anatole and Mlle Bourienne. **ROSEANNE CARRARA**

The motivations of Kuragins and Drubetskoys: Tolstoy sees the trajectory of families in society as biological organisms (as he does with armies). A Darwinian struggle for survival (social, financial advancement)—at times it's dispassionate and chilling. **FARISA KHALID**

Like a virus, for instance? **TERESA FINN**

How To Tell a True War Story, the Nikolai Rostov edition: *"He began his story meaning to tell everything just as it happened, but imperceptibly, involuntarily, and inevitably he lapsed into falsehood."* **MATT GALLAGHER**

Rostov recounting his Schöngraben action in the way *"those who take part in battles usually tell them... in the way they would like it to have been... but not at all the way it had been"* reminds me of my father's stories about Vietnam. **ZULMA ORTIZ-FUENTES**

"Rostov remembered what reply he should have given only when the man was already gone. And he was the more angry because he had forgotten to say it."
I feel so called out. **AURELIA DRAKE**

"Both had changed greatly since they last met and both were in a hurry to show the changes that had taken place in them."
Tolstoy is a genius at encapsulating emotional states throughout life, this scene is so evocative of young adulthood. **KATE CORDES**

"And so it was decided to send the letters and money by the Grand Duke's courier to Boris and Boris was to forward them to Nicholas."
The time it took for love and care to travel back then. Pre Venmo, pre email, what an uncertain yet hopeful world that was back then. **KENNY SUI-FUNG YIM**

DAY 18
APRIL 4

YIYUN LI

START
Volume I,
Part Three, VIII
"On the day after
the meeting"

END
Volume I,
Part Three, IX
"remained for
a time with the
Izmailovsk
regiment."

A third [adjutant] was playing a Viennese waltz on the piano-
forte, a fourth was lying on the pianoforte and singing along.

Unnamed characters and their mysteries: Is the singer facing
upward, or is he facing the pianist, watching his fingers?

—

Prince Andrei always became especially animated when he
had to guide a young man and help him towards worldly
success. Under the pretext of this help for another, which out of
pride he would never accept for himself, he found himself close
to the milieu which conferred success and which attracted him.

If I were Prince Andrei, I would prefer to be written by anyone
but Tolstoy.

—

What precision... what foresight of all possibilities, all condi-
tions, all the smallest details!... The combination of Austrian
clarity and Russian courage—what more do you want?

Perhaps a dose of uncertainty, as Napoleon had before the battle?

THAT'S WHAT THAT WAS ABOUT! WHO KNEW!

A professor in graduate school said there is nothing like reading a great novel for the first time. Once read, you can never regain the mystery. Don't treat this slow unwinding thrill lightly, he told us. Every sentence...

Douglas Day, a student of Faulkner's at the University of Virginia, novelist, male model, Hemingway hero. He founded the university's Latin American literature program. I miss him. MISS MAINWARING

> I find rereading even better. Keener sense of all the details, parallels, irony, character, relationship development—everyone feels more like family. There's less mystery with plot, but more in the wonder of this world. MOLLY ELIZABETH PORTER

> Ah but the innocent unravelling. Being led blind by the prose. You're talking about analysis, understanding how it works and maybe why. He was talking about the magic of unknowing. MISS MAINWARING

> Fair, though I think there's also a joy of discovery when you're not as concerned with plot. MOLLY ELIZABETH PORTER

> I was thinking about this while gardening. Seeing a painting for the first time, revisiting it, also studying it. The first time is just me trusting the art to tell me, only me, something. MISS MAINWARING

> I've taught some books thirty times. There is always new insight, connection, wonder. But the personal experience and joy of letting a new story unfold is like falling in love. TERESA FINN

> Thirty times! I wonder if you reread them every year, or whether the stories flow through your veins by now. MOLLY ELIZABETH PORTER

> I think about most of them every day. I say, "Oh! That's what that was about! Who knew!" TERESA FINN

DAY 19
APRIL 5

START
Volume I, Part
Three, X
"At dawn on
the sixteenth"

END
Volume I, Part
Three, XIII
"worthy of my
people, you,
and myself.
Napoleon."

As in a clock the result of the complex movement of numberless wheels and pulleys is merely the slow and measured movement of the hands pointing to the time, so also the result of all the complex human movements of these hundred and sixty thousand Russians and French—all the passions, desires, regrets, humiliations, sufferings, bursts of pride, fear, rapture—was merely the loss of the battle of Austerlitz, the so-called battle of the three emperors, that is, a slow movement of the world-historical hand on the clockface of human history.

We no longer rely on clocks that need winding once a week, and are perhaps less capable of imagining ourselves as cogs and wheels and pulleys. We are as omnipotent as our digital devices.

—

Kutuzov: *"The point of the matter was to satisfy the irresistible human need for sleep."*

Rostov: *"Trying to fight off the sleep that was irresistibly overcoming him."*

The most experienced and the most inexperienced fall asleep the night before the battle.

—

The reading (in German... over an hour...) of the disposition: I have a fantasy of gathering a Zoomful of people to act out the scene. I can do the *"significant gaze, which signified nothing."*

Got up late—jaded. The same sadness. Particularly now at the sight of everyone at home. The cleaners are polishing the floor; we made it dirty. I've let myself go and am less strict with myself.

LEO TOLSTOY (APRIL 5, 1884)

YIYUN LI

START
Volume I,
Part Three, XIV
"At five o'clock in
the morning"

END
Volume I,
Part Three, XVI
"'And thank
God!'..."

A soldier in movement is as hemmed in, limited, and borne along by his regiment as a sailor by his ship. However far he may go, whatever strange, unknown, and dangerous latitudes he gets into, around him—as for the sailors always and everywhere there are the same decks, masts, and rigging of his ship—always and everywhere there are the same comrades, the same ranks, the same sergeant major Ivan Mitrich, the same company dog Zhuchka, the same superiors.

"*Always and Everywhere*"—the most comforting words, even if unsustainable; and the most ominous words, though overly sensational—would make a grander title for a novel than "War and Peace."

—

When the sun had fully emerged... [Napoleon] took the glove from his beautiful white hand, made a sign to the marshals, and gave the order for the action to begin.

Tolstoy gives some of the best gestures in the novel to Napoleon, starting with the shedding of a single glove as an historical beginning.

—

Prince Andrei could not look with indifference at the standards of the battalions going past him. Looking at a standard, he thought: maybe it is that very standard with which I'll have to march at the head of the troops.

The standard: not so different from a Russian prince in Mlle Bourienne's fantasy, or a husband in Princess Marya's.

THE NOVEL BY ADRIENNE RICH

All winter you went to bed early, drugging yourself on *War and Peace*

Prince Andrei's cold eyes taking in the sky from the battlefield

were your eyes, you went walking wrapped in his wound

like a padded coat against the winds from the two rivers

You went walking in the streets as if you were ordinary

as if you hadn't been pulling with your raw mittened hand

on the slight strand that held your tattered mind

blown like an old stocking from a wire

on the wind between two rivers.

                               All winter you asked nothing

of that book though it lay heavy on your knees

you asked only for a shed skin, many skins in which to walk

you were old woman, child, commander

you watched Natasha grow into a neutered thing

you felt your heart go still while your eyes swept the pages

you felt the pages thickening to the left and on the right-

hand growing few, you knew the end was coming

you knew beyond the ending lay

your own, unwritten life

DAY 21
APRIL 7

YIYUN LI

START
Volume I, Part
Three, XVII
"At nine o'clock"

END
Volume I, Part
Three, XIX
"handed over
to the care
of the local
inhabitants."

One could see the puffs of gunsmoke as if running and chasing each other on the slopes, and the smoke of the cannon swirling, spreading, and merging together. One could see, from the gleam of bayonets amidst the smoke, the moving masses of infantry and the narrow strips of artillery with green caissons.

If one could suspend imagining what comes next, one could fall for the inhuman beauty of an advancing troop.

—

On the narrow dam of Augesd, on which for so many years an old miller in a cap used to sit peacefully with his fishing rods, while his grandson, his shirtsleeves rolled up, fingered the silvery, trembling fish in the watering can; on this dam over which, for so many years, Moravians in shaggy hats and blue jackets had peacefully driven in their two-horse carts laden with wheat and had driven back over the same dam all dusty with flour, their carts white—now, on this narrow dam, between wagons and cannon, under horses and between wheels, crowded men disfigured by the fear of death, crushing each other, dying, stepping over the dying, and killing each other, only to go a few steps and be killed themselves just the same.

One hears the echo of this passage in Isaac Babel's stories and Hemingway's novels.

—

Napoleon, as the victor, was *"happy in the unhappiness of others."* Is that better or worse than someone who's unhappy in the happiness of others?

NAPOLEON'S EYES

"Looking into Napoleon's eyes, Prince Andrei thought about the insignificance of grandeur, about the insignificance of life, the meaning of which no one could understand, and about the still greater insignificance of death..."
A novel this BIG can hold THAT. JULIA AZAR RUBIN

When Napoleon presumes Prince Andrei is dead, Andrei *"heard these words as if he was hearing the buzzing of a fly."* It's impossible not to think of Emily Dickinson: "I heard a Fly buzz—when I died—" ELLIOTT HOLT

Prince Andrei meets Napoleon and is too paralyzed by injuries to become the Russian superhero he dreams of by killing Napoleon—we might flash back to Anna Pavlovna's opening soiree, where the vicomte tells the anecdote of a duke facing a paralyzed Napoleon, also unable to kill. BRIAN OLSON

Close to death, Prince Andrei believes he knew *"nothing till now."* On the face of a victorious Napoleon is *"the radiance of self-satisfaction and happiness."*
War rests entirely on illusions; the winners maintain theirs. MIKE LEVINE

The futility of war—the redheaded gunner and the French soldier fighting over a mop! PAUL SERVINI

Even in the midst of a bloody battle, Tolstoy allows us to see the smallest of details and these images stay with us: *"Only a little soil crumbled down the bank from the horse's hind hoofs."* LAURA SPENCE-ASH

War and Peace so far: About how men struggle to stay relevant as they age, one of history's most common mechanisms for doing so—sending someone else's kid to war. JON LITTLE

"He felt afraid—afraid not for his life but for the courage he needed and which he knew could not withstand the sight of all those unfortunates."
Tolstoy knows everyone's black heart. ANNIE LIONTAS

THE POINT OF VIEW OF A HORSE

The leap to the point of view of the horse, utterly indifferent to human dreams of glory, is one of my favorite things in Part Three. It reminds me of the crazy and harrowing horse point of view in *Germinal*. Other great horse points of view in literature? (Do Achilles's weeping horses count?) **GARTH GREENWELL**

Don't forget Tolstoy's shift to the dog in *Anna Karenina*! **JOSHUA BARONE**

Laska! **MOLLY ELIZABETH PORTER**

Have you read "I, Loshad" by Jiri Kratochvil? It's from *Best European Fiction 2012*. Really outstanding, memorable story, completely from the point of view of a horse! **JOSEPH SCAPELLATO**

William Maxwell enters dog point of view in *So Long, See You Tomorrow*. **ELLEN PRENTISS CAMPBELL**

John Hawkes, one of my all-time favorites, has a book called *Sweet William: A Memoir of Old Horse*; the book is told from the point of view of the horse—it's wonderful. **CHARLES KELL**

I think my favorite passage of Cormac McCarthy's is in *The Crossing* when he switches to the point of view of the wolf. **KEVIN GEORGAS**

And then there's the lion in "The Short Happy Life of Francis Macomber." **ANN PACKER**

Also see Jaimy Gordon's great horserace novel, *Lord of Misrule*. **JOHN DOMINI**

I think David Malouf has a donkey POV in his exquisite novella *Ransom*, a retelling of Priam's journey to Achilles to get the body of Hector back. The donkey's name is Beauty. **TIM BYRNE**

I have found that the more uncertain life is, the more solidity and structure Tolstoy's novels provide. In these times, one does want to read an author who is so deeply moved by the world that he could appear unmoved in his writing.

YIYUN LI

VOLUME
TWO

YIYUN LI

START
Volume II,
Part One, I
"At the
beginning
of 1806"

END
Volume II,
Part One, IV
"Everyone
was silent."

The footman Prokofy, the one who was so strong he could lift a carriage by the back rail, was plaiting slippers out of cloth trimmings.

Carriage lifting and slipper plaiting: either makes him a real character; together they make him unforgettable.

—

Rostov again entered that world of his family and childhood... and the burning of the arm with a ruler to show love did not seem nonsense to him; he understood and was not surprised at it.

The terrifying power of a childhood home supports Hegel: What is rational is actual; and what is actual is rational.

—

Yes, he's very handsome.... I know him. For him there would be a special charm in disgracing my name and laughing at me, precisely because I solicited for him, took him in, and helped him.... Yes, he's a duellist... to kill a man is nothing to him. He must think everybody's afraid of him, it must make him feel good. He must think I'm also afraid of him. And, in fact, I am afraid of him.

Pierre is more clear-eyed than most characters in the novel, despite behaving like a bumblebee: he assesses Dolokhov as Tolstoy dissects Prince Andrei, and doesn't allow the thinnest veil of self-deception when admitting his fear of Dolokhov.

HOW STORIES GET REWRITTEN

"When the news began to filter through, there was virtually a conspiracy of silence—not a word was spoken about the war and the latest defeat.... Moscow society sensed that things were going wrong, but bad news was painful to dwell on, so they kept quiet. But it wasn't long before the bigwigs re-emerged like jurymen from a jury room..."

Tolstoy keeps showing how stories get rewritten. The Muscovites celebrate Bagration for leading an orderly retreat while holding off a force twice his size at Austerlitz. **THOMAS J. KITSON**

This has been the default position of fiction: things turn out different from expected, character is contradiction, etc. **AMITAVA KUMAR**

The more I read, the less I know. **KENNY SUI-FUNG YIM**

One of my favorite things about this novel. **ANSER**

Reading *War and Peace* is like falling into a kaleidoscope. How it expands and contracts and then keeps expanding and contracting out beyond itself into all the other books I've loved. **MISS MAINWARING**

Pierre is always distracted, unconsciously listening to a logic earworm he doesn't understand. Even preparing for a duel, *"Pierre had the look of a man occupied with some considerations of no concern to the present affair."* **ANDRÉE GREENE**

"'If only I could escape, run away and bury myself somewhere,' came the persistent thought. But whenever such ideas arose in his mind he would assume a kind of tranquility and detachment that commanded respect in the onlookers."

No one ever said reading Tolstoy wasn't without its dangers. A bee stung me as I read outside and, without thinking, I flung the book. Somehow appropriate to begin Volume II with scars. **ISAAC ZISMAN**

DAY 23
APRIL 9

START
Volume II,
Part One, V
"'Well, begin!'
said Dolokhov."

END
Volume II,
Part One, X
"dinners,
evening parties,
and balls."

YIYUN LI

Dolokhov, the *"rowdy duellist, lived in Moscow with his old mother and hunchbacked sister, and was a most affectionate son and brother."*

The girl has only three words given to her. "The Hunchbacked Sister" would be a perfect title for a novella.

—

The wheel went on turning by inertia. Princess Marya long remembered the dying creak of the wheel, which merged for her with what followed after.

When the news of a death arrives, there is always a wheel spinning, or a phone ringing, or a bee buzzing, unaware of its destined connection to forever.

—

Seeing the prince lying on the sofa, Tikhon looked at him, at his upset face, shook his head, silently went over to him, kissed him on the shoulder, and went out without tending to the candles or saying why he had come.

Not everyone deserves a Tikhon in their lives; every Tikhon deserves a Tolstoy.

AWAITING A CHILD

If the jury is still out on Natasha—frivolous schoolgirl or old soul?—her instinctive distrust of Dolokhov makes a strong case for the latter. BOB HILLMAN

This juror has already decided she's an old soul! ROBERT DEAM TOBIN

It definitely made me like her even more. She had previously also read Pierre quite astutely. AURELIA DRAKE

In some areas of early modern Europe, a woman's lifetime risk of dying in childbirth was a staggering one in three. If you had ten children you were spinning the roulette wheel ten times. MARGARET HARRIS

It's always chilling for me to read these terrible birth scenes, because I know my fate would have been the same: I spent four days in and out of labor with my first child, and only made it through thanks to an emergency C-section. Lise's end was all too common. AURELIA DRAKE

I can't help but blame the German doctor for Lise's death. After all, he has no name. MISS MAINWARING

"Following the belief that the less people know about the suffering of a woman in labor the less she suffers."
One way we cope with suffering that we ourselves are not going through. PAMELA ERENS

What. A. Scene. Death is senseless, but so is life, perhaps wonderfully so. MOLLY ELIZABETH PORTER

Birth unnerves the characters but not the author. Silence reigns, and superstition. Three times Tolstoy evokes the *"presence of the unfathomable"*—he too has sat silent in those halls, awaiting a child. ALIX CHRISTIE

Tolstoy on childbirth—such a simple, elegant sentence in a loud, tragic set of chapters, but it's what lingered with me most today: *"The most solemn mystery in the world continued its course."* MATT GALLAGHER

DAY 24
APRIL 10

START
Volume II,
Part One, XI
"On the third day
of Christmas"

END
Volume II,
Part One, XVI
"which was
already in
Poland."

YIYUN LI

The girls at Iogel's balls: *"All of them, with rare exceptions, were or seemed pretty."*

Is there a less charitable verb than that *"seemed"*? I feel like taking up a sewing needle as my sabre and challenging that fine word.

—

At that moment his life at home—jokes with Petya, talks with Sonya, duets with Natasha, piquet with his father, and even his quiet bed in the house on Povarskaya—presented itself to him with such force, clarity, and delight, as though it were all a long past, lost, and unappreciated happiness.

Losing at the card game gives Nikolai the same epiphany as the lofty sky gives Prince Andrei, though being destroyed slowly by a friend is a hundred times more terrifying than dying on the battleground. (And terrifying to watch, too.)

—

Dolokhov plays until Nikolai owes him 43,000 rubles *"because forty-three made up the sum of his age plus Sonya's."*

It's better to have *"a wicked and unfeeling man"* (Natasha has good intuition), who operates with adolescent melodrama, as an enemy rather than a friend.

FORMS OF LOVE

After a few too many glasses of wine, I almost took a day off today. Rewarded by various forms of love. Fatherly love. Young, evanescent love. Cynical love: *"No, but listen—I've been in love thousands of times, and I shall be again and again."* **MIKE PALINDROME**

Tolstoy knows the inner heart of youth. As soon as Natasha came into the room, she fell in love not *"with anyone in particular, but in love with everyone."* This is true freedom. **ANNIE LIONTAS**

The power and class dynamics in Moscow are so different than they are on campaign—he's a bit of a creeper, I know, but I still felt for Denisov. Good enough to lead the Rostov's son in combat, good enough to entertain them, but marry their daughter? Heaven forbid. **MATT GALLAGHER**

"Only on horseback and in the mazurka did Denisov's small stature not show, and he looked like the fine fellow he felt himself to be." **ANTHONY DOMESTICO**

Dancing in spurs! Bravo Denisov! **MISS MAINWARING**

A coming-of-age moment for the young Rostov during the card game: *"I was so happy, so free, so light-hearted. And I didn't even know then how happy I was."* **ROBERT P. DROUIN**

When we first meet Dolokhov in the high window, he seems like an impulsive daredevil. Natasha fills out the portrait: He's unnatural, without feeling. All the risks he takes are carefully weighed; there's nothing spontaneous about him. He's the devil playing for Nikolai's soul. **THOMAS J. KITSON**

Nikolai's *"stupid nonchalant smile for which he was long unable to forgive himself"*—so devastating in English, I couldn't bear to read it in Russian. **ANNIE LIONTAS**

How much is 43,000 rubles? Earlier, a top-quality horse cost 1,000 rubles. So 43 very good horses. Maybe the modern equivalent is 43 posh cars (in a country where the gap between rich and poor is vast). **MICHAEL G. FAULKNER**

DAY 25
APRIL 11

START
Volume II,
Part Two, I
"After his talk
with his wife"

END
Volume II,
Part Two, III
"with joy and
tender feeling."

YIYUN LI

Pierre and his Masonic pursuit: I'm delighted to realize that for the three chapters we read today, I have zero Post-its on the pages. (For other chapters I don't do so well at counting the Post-its.)

—

His servant handed him a book cut as far as the middle, an epistolary novel by Mme Souza.

A new book cut *"as far as the middle"* is a curious detail: Who cut it? (The servant?) Why only half? (Does he not have confidence in the book?)

—

Pierre's conversation with the Mason reminds me of overhearing my husband respectfully explaining to a proselytizer at our door:

> "I'm trained as a scientist, and I don't think I can say with 100 percent certainty that I know something."

> The man replied: "That's the difference. You can't say you know the truth, but we can."

I WANT WITH ALL MY HEART

Wow these Freemason chapters are terrible. So was Andrei's schlocky resurrection just in time for Lise—whom suddenly he realizes he loves—to die. If Susan Lucci isn't in the cast I don't want this hetero melodrama! Relieved to know Tolstoy had bad days too. GARTH GREENWELL

Two different crises of spirit: In the midst of battle and imminent mortality, Andrei loses himself contemplating infinity in the sky. In the emotional shambles that follow infidelity, Pierre confronts the mystery of existence, the idea of pure life through the Masons. WAYNE SCOTT

Not even a third of the way through *War and Peace* and all the principal male characters have been utterly destroyed by getting what they wanted (money, marriage, battle, etc.). Now they're searching for the next thing that will fix them. BENJAMIN T. MILLER

"What is bad? What is good? What should one love, what hate? Why live, and what am I? What is life, what is death?" And his answer *"You will die—and everything will end."*
 Pierre's existential crisis. Poor man. ZULMA ORTIZ-FUENTES

A favorite passage: *"Everything within him and around him seemed confused, senseless, and loathsome. But in this very loathing for everything around him, Pierre took a sort of irritating pleasure."* ANTHONY DOMESTICO

"I want with all my heart to be what you would want me to be."
 Pierre the enthusiast is often eager to live up to others' convictions; he wants so badly to participate, even when he has grave doubts: *"He was afraid not to believe him."* THOMAS J. KITSON

An interesting aspect of these chapters for me: Pierre was *"unused to speaking about abstract subjects in Russian."* AURELIA DRAKE

Pierre can only remember six of the seven steps as he joins the Masons. If he had paid attention to Mozart's *Magic Flute*, he would know the seventh! Don't talk! There are whole songs in the opera about keeping quiet!
ROBERT DEAM TOBIN

DAY 26
APRIL 12

START
Volume II,
Part Two, IV
"Soon after
that it was
not the
rhetor"

END
Volume II,
Part Two, VII
"an intimate
of Countess
Bezukhov's
house."

YIYUN LI

Won't I be ashamed to remember it?

Pierre's thought about the Masonic rituals reminds me of when, at almost four years old, I couldn't cry at the memorial service for Chairman Mao. Instead of mourning, I looked around at other kids, and was caught by a teacher.

—

There are two thermometers in Anna Pavlovna's drawing room: Napoleon as a political villain, and Pierre as a spoiled and depraved idiot.

—

Boris smiled cautiously, so that his smile could be understood either as mockery or as approval of the joke, depending on how it was received.

I've been wrong to think it's boring to have my characters smile—it's my fault if their smile is empty.

A CATALOG OF SMILES

PIERRE *"smiled. His smile was unlike the half-smile of other people. When he smiled, his grave, even rather gloomy, look was instantaneously replaced by another—a childlike, kindly, even rather silly look, which seemed to ask forgiveness."*

ANDREI *"with a scarcely perceptible smile which showed that, in spite of all his love and respect for his father, he was aware of his weaknesses"* and *"with a smile that showed that his father's foibles did not prevent his son from loving and honoring him."*

NIKOLAI *"unable to repress the smile of delight induced by his ride and especially by the sound of the bullets."*

SONYA *"considered it proper to show an interest in the general conversation by smiling, but in spite of herself... her smile could not for a single instant impose upon anyone."*

DOLOKHOV *"wore no mustache, so that his mouth, the most striking feature of his face, was clearly seen... and something like two distinct smiles played continually round the two corners of the mouth."*

"But the smile did not enhance VERA*'s beauty as smiles generally do; on the contrary it gave her an unnatural, and therefore unpleasant, expression."*

HÉLÈNE *"smiled, with a look implying that she did not admit the possibility of anyone seeing her without being enchanted."*

KUTUZOV *"smiled in a way that seemed to say, 'You are quite at liberty not to believe me and I don't even care whether you do or not, but you have no grounds for telling me so. And that is the whole point.'"*

NATASHA said *"'That's me from now on! I'm never going to get married. I'm going to be a ballet dancer'... and tiptoed out of the room like a ballerina, but she was smiling the smile of a happy fifteen-year-old girl."*

MARYA... has not yet smiled?

DAY 27
APRIL 13

START
Volume II,
Part Two, VIII
"The war was
heating up"

END
Volume II,
Part Two, X
"that is, all
they could."

FOR

I'm just going to say it: I like Prince Andrei.

Andrei is resolute to the point of rigidity. That's his problem. But I love that he can be changed by experience: war, death of his wife, birth of his child. Pierre is muddled, lapsed, uselessly existentialist. That's his problem.

ALEXANDRA SCHWARTZ

AGAINST

"It was not what he read in the letter that made him angry; what made him angry was that the life there, now foreign to him, could excite him."

I keep having an allergic reaction to Prince Andrei, instead of simply being made ill or being made to feel better. (It must be a sign of a successful character.)

YIYUN LI

YIYUN LI

START
Volume II,
Part Two, XI
"Returning
from his
southern
journey"

END
Volume II,
Part Two, XV
"Rostov
noticed tears
in Denisov's
eyes."

Old Prince Bolkonsky speaks of Pierre: *"Another man talks cleverly, and you don't want to listen to him, but he talks nonsense, yet he fires me up, old as I am."* Then he says to Pierre: *"I'll come and sit with you at supper. And argue again. Love my foolish Princess Marya."*

Pierre makes Princess Marya, who's embarrassed all the time, feel comfortable. Here, he makes old Prince Bolkonsky, who's often angry and cruel, speak with kindness—possibly the only time in the novel he does so. One has to adore Pierre for his effect on people.

—

I wondered what Tolstoy's contemporaries felt about the novel. Turgenev, who had a falling out with Tolstoy, complained often in his letters when he reached where we are in the book.

> Tolstoy startles the reader with the tip of [Tsar] Aleksandr's shoe, or with Speranski's laugh, making one believe that the author, having deciphered such trifles, knows everything.... And how agonizing are the premeditated and stubborn repetitions of one and the same brush stroke—the downy upper lip of Princess [Lise] Bolkonski, etc.

I—ahem—agree fully with Turgenev (but I can't seem to find his Twitter handle). **MARK TERCEK**

A few days later, still pondering *War and Peace*, Turgenev wrote:

> It contains intolerable things and astonishing things, and the astonishing things, which essentially predominate, are magnificent; none of us has written anything better.

A LONG BOND

What is there not to love in the long bond of two men, who meet after life has changed them, and can discuss with honesty and depth: What is true and good? How do we live our lives? I love the friend space between them where they can be altered by each other's words. **WAYNE SCOTT**

Sometimes I wish I could escape the clutches of irony long enough to have a conversation about the purpose of life like Andrei and Pierre did. Then I get distracted by an article about the top ten things only nineties kids understand and forget all about it. **KIRTAN NAUTIYAL**

Both Andrei and Pierre have spent much of the novel brooding in isolation (today we'd call it toxic masculinity). So when they open up to one another—about belief or love, especially—it's raw and sincere, free of ulterior motives. **MATT GALLAGHER**

The contrasts between Pierre and Andrei are very unsubtle in chapter XI, but very productive. They remind us that Pierre is the character we see constantly reborn, while Andrei is the character who dies again and again. **THOMAS J. KITSON**

"It involuntarily occurred to Pierre that these thoughts had been suggested to Prince Andrei by his father. He made no reply."
A rare moment of tact from someone who does not normally seem self-conscious about his social interactions. **ROBERT DEAM TOBIN**

The two best therapists I ever had sounded just like Prince Andrei. ie., beware of doing good. It is rarely good. **MISS MAINWARING**

"In the hospitals death was such a certainty that soldiers sick with fever and bloated from bad food preferred to go on serving, forcing themselves to drag their feet to the front rather than go to the hospital."
My great-grandfather survived the 1918 flu pandemic when he was in France because, the story goes, his friends hid him in a truck and cared for him so he wouldn't get taken to a hospital. **MEGAN CUMMINS**

DAY 29
APRIL 15

START
Volume II,
Part Two, XVI
"In the month
of April"

END
Volume II,
Part Two, XXI
"'Hey, you!
Another bottle!'
he shouted."

YIYUN LI

Denisov and Rostov's dugout, with dirt steps as anteroom and broken glass as skylight, reminds me that in the army, our commander once had a bed made for her from a butcher's block borrowed from a village kitchen. A luxury that birthed many jokes.

—

"I've had a bit cut off, see..." he said, smiling and showing the empty sleeve of the robe.

Seeing Tushin again (alive! still smiling! minus an arm...) puts me into a strange and familiar mood, once named by a friend as: happysad.

—

Since the time of his entrance into the higher world, Boris had made it his habit to observe attentively what was happening around him and to write it down.... At the moment when the emperors went into the pavilion, he looked at his watch, and he did not forget to look again when Alexander came out of the pavilion. The meeting had lasted an hour and fifty-three minutes; and he wrote it down that evening, among other facts which he supposed were of historic significance.

Chroniclers are only footnotes in world events. But in Tolstoy's fiction they blossom into a character like Boris, whose ambition is to inset his posterity into history.

THE ACT OF READING

One day I had a reading experience that greatly disturbed me and still does to this day. I must have been coming back from vacation, either from Italy or from the Côte d'Azur, I can't remember at all. What I know is that I had to take a train that was leaving very early in the morning and would arrive in Paris at night. I had very little luggage, mainly consisting of a canvas bag and a book. The book was enormous, it was one of a pair in the Pléaide collection. One thing is certain, which is that I had not yet read this book, that I was supposed to read it on vacation, that I hadn't done so and that now I had to read it very quickly, as quickly as possible, without delay. Because, for one, I had promised both to read it and to return it on a specific date that must have been the day after I returned from vacation, and, for another, if my promise was not kept, no other book would be lent to me from then on. I don't have any idea why my book lender was so strict, but even if it wasn't true, I absolutely believed it, I believed I had to do it or else I would have no more books to read. I didn't have the money to buy them and I didn't dare steal them. The stakes were enormous.

The train left. Immediately I began to read the first line of the tragic book. I continued. I must not have eaten during the journey, and when the train arrived at the Gare de Lyon it was late at night. The train had probably been delayed, daylight was already gone. I had read eight hundred pages of *War and Peace* in a day: half of the book. The memory of that journey took a long time to fade. For a while it felt like a betrayal of the act of reading. Thinking about it again today, it still disturbs me. Something had been sacrificed in my rapid reading of the book, perhaps another kind of reading. I clung to a reading of the story told in the book at the expense of a deep and white reading without any narration, a reading of the pure writing of Tolstoy. It's as if I had realized that day and forever after that a book was contained bewteen two layers superimposed with writing, the legible lyaer that I had read that day as I traveled and the other, inaccessible. That layer, completely unreadable, we can only get an inkling of its existence when we're distracted from a literal reading, the way we glimpse childhood through a child. It would take forever to explain it and it wouldn't be worth the effort.

But I never forgot *War and Peace*.... What still lingers from that day is the image of a train crossing over a plain.... And the memory, not so much of Tolstoy as of my betrayal of his entire being. **MARGUERITE DURAS**

DAY 30
APRIL 16

YIYUN LI

START
Volume II,
Part Three, I
"In 1808 the em-
peror Alexander
went"

END
Volume II,
Part Three, V
"trying not to be
noticed, left the
room."

As soon as he opened the shutters, moonlight, as if it had been watching at the window a long time waiting for that, burst into the room... Just under his window was a row of trimmed trees, black on one side and silvery bright on the other... He could hear the rustle of her dress and even her breathing.

Tolstoy gives the most romantic moment of the novel to Prince Andrei, the least romance-minded character. (Like slipping one of Falstaff's lines into King Lear's script with the uttermost ease.)

—

Prince Andrei has his *"huge, gnarled, ungainly... old, angry, scornful, and ugly"* oak tree.

Jane Eyre has her lightning-struck chestnut tree, "split down the centre... ghastly."

I have in front of my window a young dogwood tree, blossoming unobtrusively.

—

Prince Andrei is *"an eligible young man, rich and well-born... with the aura of the romantic story of his alleged death and his wife's tragic end."*

A wife's death, an honor earned from the domestic battleground, can be as valuable a decoration in society as the Saint Andrew's honor earned from war.

REAL LIFE

My old copy has this delightful footnote with an anecdote from Tolstoy's early life... this editor was having fun:

> Natásha's fancy tallies with one Tolstóy himself had at the age of seven or eight. Under its influence he actually threw himself out of a window some eighteen feet from the ground. He was picked up unconscious. This resulted in a slight concussion of the brain, but after sleeping eighteen hours on end he recovered and experienced no further ill effect. **MOLLY ELIZABETH PORTER**

As a fifty-eight-year-old, I was enjoying Andrei's rejuvenation, the *"juicy green leaves"* breaking though *"the stiff, hundred-year-old bark."* Then Andrei says, *"No, life isn't over at the age of thirty-one"*! Tolstoy! Thirty-one isn't old! **ROBERT DEAM TOBIN**

A great oak transforming and a woman's spirit help Andrei out of himself. It's a wonderful scene, full of warmth and hope. Andrei evolving into a mensch. *"Your father, a man of the old days"*—the Russians knew old school. The Bolkonskys are my favorite *War and Peace* people. **SALVADOR ORTEGA**

I'm enjoying the contrast of the Rostovs and Bolkonskys as the rarities they are—relatively happy families. **MISS MAINWARING**

"Life, meanwhile, people's real life, with its essential concerns of health, illness, work, rest, with its concerns of thought, learning, poetry, music, love, friendship, hatred, passions, went on as always."
Almost a summary of quarantine life. **MICHAEL G. FAULKNER**

DAY 31
APRIL 17

START
Volume II,
Part Three, VI
"During the initial
time of his stay in
Petersburg"

END
Volume II,
Part Three, X
"if Thou forsakest
me altogether."

He felt that the further the ground he stood on gave way under his feet, the more involuntarily he was bound to it.

Pierre's Masonic career is less memorable than his feeling about it—any decision one makes seems capable of becoming that ground.

—

I once said in a lecture that omniscient Tolstoy didn't have any character dreaming in *War and Peace*. I was wrong. I forgot he let Pierre write about his own dreams in his diary. If someone bores us by recounting dreams, of course it would be poor Pierre.

—

Pierre prays to God for help *"to overcome the part of wrath by gentleness and slowness."*
    Slowness as a virtue is fascinating. Slow in what way? Thinking? Feeling? Challenging someone to a duel? Reading Tolstoy?

ANSWERS IN OTHERS

Men in *War and Peace* look for answers in others (Rostov's worship of the tsar; Andrei's respect for Bonaparte and Speransky; Pierre and the Masons) until they are disillusioned enough to look within. Just as Russia stops looking abroad, finds its own identity. **ELLIOTT HOLT**

Pierre's diary entries are so heartbreaking. Usually Tolstoy's narration gives the reader a kind of protective, loving, even sometimes humorous distance from his pain and confusion—one I only appreciated when this epistolary section stripped that distance. **OLIVIA WOLFGANG-SMITH**

> Tolstoy really laying it on thick with this detail of Pierre's obviously subpar diaristic tendencies. **GENEVIEVE WOLLENBECKER**

Pierre, for all his false starts in striving for self-improvement and incompetently executed goodwill so far, lives a life very much worth living, a self-examined life. There is intrinsic value in this of itself, we see more and more. **JOHN NEELEMAN**

Andrei, teaching his three-course semester: *"He sometimes noticed with displeasure that he had happened to repeat the same thing on the same day in different companies."* **ANTHONY DOMESTICO**

Andrei and Pierre, such struggles. I want to scream at them both! **ZULMA ORTIZ-FUENTES**

I love how casually Tolstoy zeroes in on a particular form of arrogance, then moves on to another paragraph and topic... *"of reason, and flattering him in honeyed tones bordering on the kind of arrogance that exists in a tacit assumption between two men that they are the only people capable of appreciating how stupid* everybody else *is and how wise and profound their own thoughts are."* **CARL PHILLIPS**

Every evening over cocktails, my husband and I have *"a tacit assumption that one's companion is the only man besides oneself capable of understanding the folly of the rest of mankind and the reasonableness and profundity of one's own ideas."* **REBECCA MIRSKY**

YIYUN LI

START
Volume II,
Part Three, XI
"The financial
affairs of the
Rostovs"

END
Volume II,
Part Three, XV
"'the way he
does with
these ladies.'"

It was as if they were ashamed that they loved Vera so little and were now so eager to get her off their hands.

"Unquestionably beautiful and sensible," and unloved and uncourted by anyone but Berg: poor Vera sounds like a changeling.

—

Natasha's observation of Boris—*"he's so narrow, like a dining-room clock"*—corroborates Turgenev's comment on Tolstoy—"he hates sober-mindedness, system, and science (in a word, German)."

—

Natasha *"speaking of herself in the third person and imagining that it was some very intelligent man saying it about her... 'There's everything in her, everything,' this man went on, 'she's extraordinarily intelligent, sweet, and then, too, pretty, extraordinarily pretty, nimble—she swims, she's an excellent horsewoman, and the voice!'"*

I've tried this trick, but to the opposite effect. The adjectives I come up with are not as complimentary as Natasha's.

VOWS

In which *War and Peace* appears to borrow from the giddily fatalistic determinism of the "Vows" section of the *New York Times.* *"Four years before, Berg had pointed out Vera Rostov to a German comrade he had met in the stalls of a Moscow theatre and said to him in German, 'She's going to be my wife.' That was the moment he had made up his mind to marry her. Now in Petersburg, after taking stock of the Rostovs' position and his own, he had decided the time had come to propose."* AMITAVA KUMAR

The decent, beleaguered Rostovs bring to mind Lucretius:

> Men wear themselves out to no purpose and sweat drops of blood as they struggle on along the road of ambition, since they gather their knowledge from the mouths of others and follow after hearsay. JOHN NEELEMAN

Natasha is wiser than her years. And very observant. Despite her fondness for Boris, she finds him *"gray, light grey."* While Pierre is *"blue, dark blue with red and he's rectangular."* ZULMA ORTIZ-FUENTES

The *"well-known mansion on the English Embankment blazed with countless lights."* Tolstoy sets the stage, at a réveillon where Natasha will meet the three most important men in her life! SIGRID PAUEN

The male schemers looking for a fortune are great Austen characters. And everyone loves Natasha. ANDREW BERTAINA

Everyone except Berg, who says Vera's sister is *"unpleasant."* MOLLY ELIZABETH PORTER

And so, halfway through the novel, the elaborate lead up to the ball tells us that *everything* is about to change. Just like Tchaikovsky's act-two waltz in *Eugene Onegin.* ILANN M. MAAZEL

I think I might change my name to Madame Peronsky. MISS MAINWARING

DAY 33
APRIL 19

START
Volume II,
Part Three, XVI
"Suddenly
everything
stirred"

END
Volume II,
Part Three, XXI
"and Berg
drew Pierre
into it."

YIYUN LI

Prince Andrei, like all people who have grown up in society, liked to encounter things in society that did not have the general society stamp on them.

When did old Count Bolkonsky move to the countryside? After his wife died giving birth to Marya? Marya did not grow up in society (yet she's friends with Julie Karagin). Andrei did and married one of the best society women. Backstories are rabbit holes.

—

Natasha... happy and flushed, did not stop dancing all evening. She noticed nothing and did not see any of what interested everyone at this ball. Not only did she not notice how the sovereign had a long talk with the French ambassador, how he talked with particular graciousness with a certain lady, how prince so-and-so did and said such-and-such, how Hélène had great success and was granted the special attentions of so-and-so...

Tolstoy's omniscience at its best: history and court intrigues play out in the negative space of Natasha's awareness; what she doesn't see in *"her highest degree of happiness"* is what carries the novel.

—

Berg, judging by his wife, considered all women weak and stupid. Vera, judging by her husband alone and extending the observation to everyone, supposed that all men ascribed reason only to themselves, and at the same time understood nothing, were proud and egoistic.

All happy families are alike; each unhappy family is unhappy in its own way. Judging by Berg and Vera, a good marriage is a mirror—spouses look at each other as though looking at themselves, and relish the images.

THE SALT OF MERRIMENT

How hilariously scathing Tolstoy is when describing Berg's obsession with order, his cold, calculating nature: *"He got up and kissed Vera's hand, but on his way straightened the turned-back corner of the carpet."* ELLIOTT HOLT

Vera and Berg's apartment and their "soiree" seems the perfect example of Nabokov's poshlust. The perfect symmetry, the desire only to imitate for fear of seeming unique or individual. JENNIFER SEARS

So hard you all are on poor Vera and Berg. Are they so different from Instagrammers with their interiors, dinners, children? MISS MAINWARING

Me, at "drinks": *"There was nothing bad or inappropriate in what they said, everything was witty and might have been funny; but that something which constitutes the salt of merriment was not only missing, but they did not even know it existed."* ANTHONY DOMESTICO

Andrei's response to song: *"The main thing that was bringing him to the verge of tears was a sudden, vivid awareness of the dreadful disparity between something infinitely great and eternal that existed within him and something else, something containing and physical."* HEATHER WOLF

"The main thing he wanted to weep about was a sudden, vivid awareness of the terrible opposition between something infinitely great and indefinable that was in him, and something narrow and fleshly that he himself, and even she, was. This opposition tormented and gladdened him while she sang."

Andrei falling in love with Natasha is one of the most wonderful passages I've ever read. That *"gladdened"* is unbelievably good. GARTH GREENWELL

Who'd thunk it—Andrei one of the best dancers of his time. But then I remember George Washington was also known for being a great dancer. SALVADOR ORTEGA

"Music is the shorthand of emotion. Emotions which let themselves be described in words with such difficulty, are directly conveyed to man in music, and in that is its power and significance." LEO TOLSTOY

**DAY 34
APRIL 20**

START
Volume II,
Part Three, XXII
"The next day
Prince Andrei
went to the
Rostovs'"

END
Volume II,
Part Three, XXVI
"she loved her
father and her
nephew more
than God."

YIYUN LI

Yesterday I was tormented, I suffered, but I wouldn't trade that torment for anything in the world. I've never lived before. Only now am I alive, but I can't live without her.

Even a person who never doubts his superior mind speaks of love in clichés.

—

The resemblance between Natasha and Prince Andrei, which the nanny had noticed during Prince Andrei's first visit...

A minor character immortalized by half a sentence: what the mother misses, the nanny does not.

—

It may be, I often think, that she was too angelically innocent to have the strength to bear all the duties of a mother. She was irreproachable as a young wife; perhaps she could not have been so as a mother.

Princess Marya's notion that God's infinite love for his creation made it necessary for Lise to die in childbirth: the most heartless thing I've read so far. Bloodcurdling.

TOLSTOY'S WONDERFUL JOKE

There is *War and Peace,* and there is Andrei and Pierre. Naturally, we compare these two men, who are so flagrantly, preposterously unalike, because Tolstoy tells us to. We measure Andrei's reserve and commitment to duty against Pierre's open-hearted, abstracted searching, and hold Pierre's bumbling awkwardness up to Andrei's elegant, cold detachment. But Tolstoy's wonderful joke, put into the very first scene of the novel, is that they are friends, and true ones. When Pierre shows up at Anna Pavlovna's soiree, Andrei comes alive; we see all at once that this supercilious, haughty prince has a soul. When Andrei leaves Natasha during their engagement, he tells her that she can turn to Pierre: *"He's the most absentminded and ridiculous man, but he has a heart of gold."* The men love each other, and we see each best when we look at him through the other's eyes.

A lot of readers seem to prefer Pierre. He's more modern, with his confusion and his endless existential questing; like an *X-Files* fan, he wants to believe. But Andrei's struggle with his own misplaced idealism is just as moving to me. Just before the Battle of Austerlitz, Andrei is at the council of war, listening to Russian generals discuss plans for the next day. Kutuzov thinks the battle will be lost, but won't raise objections. Andrei thinks: *"Can it really be that, for court and personal considerations, tens of thousands of lives must be risked—and my own,* my life?*"* (This uncannily captured how I felt on April 20, 2020, the day that I read it, as New York reached its coronavirus peak and the powers in Washington fiddled.) Then comes Austerlitz, with its chaos and bloody disaster. Andrei imagined that war would make him a hero. Instead, he lies near death on the corpse-strewn battlefield and, looking up at the sky, has a moment of mystical transcendence, an encounter with the infinite. When he at last glimpses Napoleon, who is surveying his army's wounded prisoners, he sees the general from a worm's point of view. *"He knew that it was Napoleon—his hero—but at that moment, Napoleon seemed to him such a small, insignificant man compared with what was now happening between his soul and this lofty, infinite sky with clouds racing across it."* Andrei is having a brush with the divine, but because we are in Tolstoy's world, the vital human element interrupts. A French soldier has nabbed the golden icon around Andrei's neck, but *"seeing the kindness with which the emperor treated the prisoners, hastened to return the icon."* That is life, selfish and repentant, interrupting death, and the transcendence Andrei has glimpsed will take him the rest of the novel to understand again.
ALEXANDRA SCHWARTZ

YIYUN LI

START
Volume II,
Part Four, I
"Biblical tradition
says that
absence
of work"

END
Volume II,
Part Four, V
"shyly smiled
his childishly
meek and
pleasant smile."

Nikolai *"had that common sense of mediocrity which told him what he* ought *to do."*

It is always the son's privilege to criticize the father: Nikolai is modeled on Tolstoy's father; Pierre and Andrei, on Tolstoy himself. Common sense, which neither Pierre nor Andrei has, is called mediocrity.

—

Though Danilo was of small stature, seeing him in the room produced an impression similar to seeing a horse or a bear standing there amidst the furniture and accessories of human life.

The serf Danilo is inimitable among the dead objects and living aristocrats.

—

There are 130 dogs at the hunt. If a dog eats healthily at 3 percent of its body weight daily, the hounds and the borzois together would consume somewhere between 150 and 200 pounds of raw meat daily. I too worry about the Rostov's finances.

WORK AND LAND

"Now a heavy curse lies upon him, not only because we have to earn our bread by the sweat of our brow, but also because our sense of morality will not allow to be both idle and at ease."

This novel is less about war and peace, for me, than work and land. The brilliance is how few characters actually work and how few care about the land. MISS MAINWARING

> Say more? How do these emerge as the major themes when they're not the preoccupations of the main characters? ROBERT BUTLER

> Working scenes are rare, but they have a special energy. Career military men. The cannoneer, Uncle the hunter, the tavern keeper who loves his tavern, Prince Bolkonsky at his desk. Even Hélène creating law. As opposed to Pierre and Andrei's existential malaise. MISS MAINWARING

> Yes, far better to spend your time being skilled at something. When the food appears at Uncle's: *"All this was the work of Anisya Fiodorovna's own hands, selected and prepared by her, and redolent of Anisya Fiodorovna herself."* ROBERT BUTLER

> Exactly! Skill, expertise, practice, handwork. The threads I'm following. MISS MAINWARING

"One of the first conditions of happiness is that the link between man and nature shall not be broken." LEO TOLSTOY

"This morning we had a visit from a 30-year-old Romanian who had castrated himself at the age of 18 after reading *The Kreutzer Sonata*. He then took to working on the land—just 19 acres—and was terribly disillusioned today to see that Tolstoy writes one thing but lives in luxury. He was obviously hurt, said he wanted to cry, kept repeating, 'My God, my God! How can this be? What shall I tell them at home?' and questioned everyone, seeking an explanation for this contradiction." SONIA TOLSTOY (AUGUST 31, 1909)

DAY 36
APRIL 22

YIYUN LI

START
Volume II,
Part Four, VI
"The old count
rode home"

END
Volume II,
Part Four, VIII
"Things were
not cheerful
in the Rostovs'
house."

Hunting is war in peace time: the wolf is a skirmish leading to the battle of the hare; Nikolai and Ilagin talking about irrelevant topics while eyeing each other's dogs is a variation of Alexander and Napoleon reviewing the two armies affably.

—

I was thinking that Rugai, the red dog, resembles uncle, and that if he were a man, he would always keep uncle with him, if not for the chase, then for his tunefulness.

Who doesn't love a tuneful dog! Nikolai, only recently called mediocre, says one of the oddest and most astonishing things in the novel. His life doesn't often allow ingenuity, but by nature he is closest to Natasha.

—

They maintained the same way of life, for without it the count and countess could not imagine life at all.

Inertia and indecisiveness are perhaps underappreciated: they do their share of life-preserving, just as imagination and action do their share of destruction.

A JOYFUL SHRIEK

"The soil in the kitchen garden, glistening wet and black as poppy seed, merged in the near distance with the dull and damp curtain of the mist... there was a smell of fading leaves and dogs."

A quiet moment of beauty before the carnage of the hunt. LAURA SPENCE-ASH

Many great episodes so far, but this wolf and hare hunt and meeting the old uncle, and the evening spent with him, his place, the food, the music, the dance... top of the list so far. The ball was pretty great, too. Writing Natasha turned Tolstoy on! MURRAY SILVERSTEIN

My favorite sequence—the wolf hunt. Like everything else in the novel, it's gory and disturbing and exciting and joyful. After reading it, I named my beloved pup Rugay. LOWELL MICK WHITE

"Natasha, without pausing for breath, let out a joyful and rapturous shriek, so shrill that it made their ears ring. With this shriek she expressed everything the other hunters had expressed with their simultaneous talk."

Natasha's uncanny shriek during the hunt. What do you hear in it? I hear fresh air, exercise, and, just maybe, liberation from the suffocation of ballrooms, talk of money, talk of marriage, and marrying for money! JEFFREY MORRIS

"'So I'm just like all the rest, when it's not a matter of the chase. Well, but when it is, watch out!' was, as it seemed to Nikolai, what the dog's look said." ANTHONY DOMESTICO

A lovely moment of *"causeless laughter"* between siblings in the uncle's study, where *"Nikolai no longer considered it necessary to display his male superiority before his sister."* As if the hunt had been all theater. ZULMA ORTIZ-FUENTES

The feast at Uncle's reminds me of my grandparents. Non's Italian food, smelling, speaking, and tasting of her. Grandpa whistling to his dog, Prince, like a bird. We'd drive home afterward, and our own house looked welcoming, alive in a different way. ROSEANNE CARRARA

One of the most
important points about
writing is the contrast
between the person
who feels poetry and
the one who doesn't.

LEO TOLSTOY

DAY 37
APRIL 23

START
Volume II,
Part Four, IX
"Christmastime
came"

END
Volume II,
Part Four, XIII
"went to Moscow
at the end of
January."

YIYUN LI

"What will I give birth to?" she asked the buffoon...
"Fleas, dragonflies, grasshoppers," the buffoon replied.

An oddly thrilling exchange (though Natasha disagrees): She's fluent in nonsense. He, with an etymologist's mind, is as nimble-witted as King Lear's clown.

—

Nikolai falls for Sonya, in a man's outfit, with a cork-drawn mustache. Sonya finds a beloved stranger in Nikolai, in a woman's dress. Seeing is disbelieving—realigning memory and desire.

Who would begrudge love between these two people, new to each other?

—

She wrote him classically monotonous, dry letters, to which she herself did not ascribe any significance, and in the drafts of which the countess corrected the spelling errors.

Oh no. A letter with spelling errors is at least less impersonal.

ON THIS DAY

Reading Tolstoy by the river today I watched an owl catch a squirrel, drop the squirrel, catch the squirrel again, drop it again, catch it a third time, then be chased off by two other squirrels. *War and Peace* seems low on drama by comparison. **GARTH GREENWELL**

"Perhaps he will come today, will come at once! Perhaps he has come and is sitting in the drawing room. Perhaps he came yesterday, and I have forgotten."
Agony, Tolstoy reminds us, exists in all tenses and expressions of time. **ANNIE LIONTAS**

"'Do you know, said Natásha in a whisper, moving closer to Nicholas and Sónya, 'that when one goes on and on recalling memories, one at last begins to remember what happened before one was in the world...'"
The Rostov kids' table rules. **NICK FULLER GOOGINS**

"Does it ever happen to you that you feel there's nothing more—nothing; that everything good has already happened? And it's not really boring, but sad?"
Natasha's lockdown ennui feels close to home. **MICHAEL G. FAULKNER**

The magic of storytelling—I worry about Natasha, imaginary savior always better than flesh and blood, flawed human. Then I feel stupid I have an emotional response for a creation of Tolstoy's imagination, 150 years ago, now expressed in little arbitrary squiggles on paper. **BRIAN OLSON**

Among the many pleasures of the Tolstoy Together group: while life has often felt on pause (which has ups and downs to it), seeing how much we've read reminds me I've been traveling all along, and not alone. **CARL PHILLIPS**

Happy I've enlisted my father. Reading the French edition, one hundred pages in, he messaged me: "Grandiose." We read together in confinement, a touching way to connect and bridge transatlantic distance. **FARAH ABDESSAMAD**

YIYUN LI

START
Volume II,
Part Five, I
"After the
engagement"

END
Volume II,
Part Five, IV
"try to get
the old prince
used to her."

It was too frightening to be under the burden of all the insoluble questions of life, and he gave himself to the first amusements that came along... but, above all, he read.

Recently my dear friend Elizabeth McCracken used the word *"insoluble"* in a note, which clarified my muddled mind instantly. Let the insoluble remain so, as long as we can say: "Above all, we read."

—

Like the old émigré who refused to marry a lady with whom he had been spending his evenings for several years, because, once married, he would not know where to spend his evenings...

What if we have a Montaigne By Oneself going at the same time—we'd have a place to go in the evening.

—

"Ah, my God, Count, there are moments when I'd marry anybody!"

Marya never expresses her eagerness to marry but to Pierre. He leads people off script—they say things that otherwise would remain unsaid, even in their private thoughts.

OUR PERIPHERAL VISION

War and Peace is the only book I've ever read that captures the richness of real life. Most novels narrow in on a handful of characters. By inventing dozens who appear in but a single scene, as in these Christmas chapters, Tolstoy restores our peripheral vision.

Most of us know people who were, for a time, at the very center of our lives, but whose importance has now faded. Tolstoy reproduces this beautifully. **MARGARET HARRIS**

Remember when we worried we wouldn't know who was who? And all the names felt impossible? **MISS MAINWARING**

Marya imagines herself as an ascetic wanderer. In 1881 Tolstoy disguised himself as a peasant and made a pilgrimage to a monastery. **MO OGRODNIK**

"It would be easier... to confide everything I feel to someone."
Opposites attract, Pierre the drunk and Marya the rigid spinster seek help and comfort from each other. **SIGRID PAUEN**

"It seemed to Pierre that all men... were seeking refuge from life: some in ambition, some in cards, some in women, in wine." Why Tolstoy always got to call me out in my existential dread? **ANNIE LIONTAS**

"Drinking wine became more and more of a physical and at the same time moral need for him.... Only when he had drunk a bottle or two of wine did he become dimly aware that the tangled, terrible knot of life, which had formerly terrified him, was not as frightening as it seemed."

There couldn't be a less Jamesian moment than when Marya says to Pierre, *"Ah, my God, Count, there are moments when I'd marry anybody!"* Such a relief to this reader, who loves Henry James, to have something that needed to be said blurted out. **TERESA FINN**

Perversely—while I both love me some Henry James and find Tolstoy's novel to be impeccably designed—his snub of *War and Peace* as a "large loose baggy monster" endears me to it all the more.
SARAH BLAKLEY-CARTWRIGHT

DAY 39
APRIL 25

YIYUN LI

START
Volume II,
Part Five, V
"Boris had failed
to marry"

END
Volume II,
Part Five, VIII
"Natasha also
began to look."

Boris had failed to marry a rich bride in Petersburg and had come with the same purpose to Moscow.

A great opening to a story. The chapter is like a play in which the actors, while performing perfectly onstage, are thinking of their suppers and nightgowns.

—

The thought of making a fool of himself and wasting this whole month of heavy melancholic duty around Julie for nothing, and seeing the income from the Penza estates, already allocated and properly put to use in his imagination, in the hands of another—especially in the hands of stupid Anatole—offended Boris.

Boris dreams too! One even feels a little touched by an unpoetic character's unpoetic imagination.

—

"It can't be that they won't come to love me... everyone has always loved me."

Natasha's hope in the Bolkonskys echoes Nikolai's shock at the French who wanted to kill him. Since when has the world stopped loving me?—a question all lucky children have to face.

THE COSTUME HIERARCHY

War and Peace may seem to hinge on many coincidences. But at the Moscow opera we see that the Russian nobility occupied a minuscule world in by some measures the most vast and diverse of nations. Not a healthy or stable condition. JOHN NEELEMAN

The peace sections are so Jane Austeny: Looking for wealthy spouses. Attending balls in beautiful dresses. Well-dressed soldiers. True love, jealousy, deceit, broken hearts. JILL TATARA

War and Peace puts the gender structures of its times under a harsh surreal light: the audience at the opera consists of *"men, old and young, in uniforms and tailcoats,"* and *"women, in precious stones on bare bodies."* ROBERT DEAM TOBIN

A striking image: the men fully clothed and the women naked. LAURA SPENCE-ASH

Tolstoy's great-grandniece, generations later still shrewdly observing appearances in Russian society:

"From the time I was a small child, you could recognize Party bigwigs and their families from a mile away because they were so proud of wearing foreign clothes," says forty-year-old writer Tatyana Tolstaya, great-grandniece of Leo Tolstoy and one of the shrewdest observers of Russian society I know. "They simply recreated the costume hierarchy we had under the czars."...

Soviet women are very candid about their fixation on costume.

"It's due to our terrible sense of bleakness..." said a program director at Riga's central television station, "decorating your outer surface is like bringing flowers inside of you, it's your only way of cheering up.... Well," she added wistfully, "it may also be due to the fact that our men don't seem to value us, don't behave toward us with any *manners.*" FRANCINE DU PLESSIX GRAY (SOVIET WOMEN: WALKING THE TIGHTROPE)

DAY 40
APRIL 26

YIYUN LI

START
Volume II,
Part Five, IX
"The stage
consisted of
flat boards"

END
Volume II,
Part Five, XIII
"no answers to
these terrible
questions."

Now the thought came to her of jumping up to the footlights and singing the aria the actress was singing, then she wanted to touch a little old man who was sitting not far away with her fan, then to lean over to Hélène and tickle her.

What would I not give to see Natasha tickle Hélène, that marble statue. Or, better, paint the statue's nose red. (One has to love a character who allows one wicked laughter.)

—

The very process of manipulating another person's will was a pleasure, a habit, and a necessity for Dolokhov.

Three plain nouns forming a terrifying crescendo. (This also reminds me of Jane Austen's line: "With them, to wish was to hope, and to hope was to expect.")

—

Hélène's dress always rustles, Anatole's spurs always jingle: We are almost certain they read nothing. Reading doesn't proclaim itself with so much fanfare.

A NIGHT AT THE OPERA

"They sang together."

Tolstoy gives us the real opera. Moving the action from stage to audience, we see the lovers perform a false duet of lust! Everybody dressing and undressing! SIGRID PAUEN

A night at the opera. Natasha realizes nobody is there for the performance—the real act is the audience. But like her brother playing cards, she doesn't realize she's the patsy at the poker table. SALVADOR ORTEGA

Tolstoy's descriptions of the opera sets—so wonderfully detached—anatomical! We see artifice as artifice in a way Natasha's just beginning to (and maybe resistant to—though she has her fantasies)—and oh to be in a crowded theater just now! ROSEANNE CARRARA

"In the second act, there were pieces of cardboard representing monuments, and there was a hole in the canvas representing the moon."

Natasha's plain descriptions of the artifice of the opera. LAURA SPENCE-ASH

When Andrei listened to Natasha from the window, moonlight invaded his room, Natasha wanted to fly to it; here, it's a hole in a cardboard. ELEONORE

The way Natasha sees the opera, as only shapes moving around, knowing what it was *"supposed to represent"* but finding it false, reminds me of Plato's allegory of the cave. AURELIA DRAKE

"She only felt herself again quite irretrievably in that strange, insane world, so far from her former one, that world in which it was impossible to know what was good, what was bad, what was sane and what insane. Behind her sat Anatole, and she, sensing his nearness, waited fearfully for something."

Please oh please oh *please* can we go back to Uncle's house and dance to the balalaika and snuggle in Anisya Fyodorovna's bosom and eat snacks and treats forever. I cannot bear the augury of Anatole I can *not*. ASH MARTIN

DAY 41
APRIL 27   YIYUN LI

START
Volume II,
Part Five, XIV
"Morning came
with its cares"

END
Volume II,
Part Five, XVII
"ran back
with him to
the troika."

Though they were all going with him, Anatole evidently wanted to make something touching and solemn out of this address to his friends.

The rehearsal for a farewell is always prettier. The real farewell, at the mercy of what's not in one's control, seldom has space for anything touching or solemn.

—

The poor horses run to their deaths by Balaga: even if they could go to a horse heaven they would still be inconsolable, next to the horses killed in the war.

—

The unnamed maid assisting Anatole in seducing Natasha: What moved her to do so? Is it money he offers, or her unbending loyalty to Natasha's wishes? Or something that defies logic and interpretation, as in life when we revisit an event we often say: I don't know why I did that.

Not knowing the maid as a reader, not knowing if she knows her own mind—often I come back to the character, and think: How you are like many people I encounter; how you are also like me.

A SCOUNDREL

Tolstoy is either parodying the sentimental novels popular in the late eighteenth century or simply indulging in a bit of soap opera himself. I cannot tell. Either way, I found myself gripped by Anatole's villainy and Natasha's "tragic heroine" bit. JEFFREY MORRIS

This Natasha-Anatole imbroglio might be my favorite episode yet. Thirty pages of cloak and dagger intrigue dedicated to one man's mission to get laid. And wherever lives are being thrown into chaos we find Dolokhov, the Napoleon of petty villainy. BENJAMIN T. MILLER

"He was met by Gabriel, Márya Dmítrievna's gigantic footman."
    May all scheming assholes find a Gabriel in their path. ADAM SNYDER

"If I don't sleep for three nights I'll not leave this passage and will hold her back by force and not let the family be disgraced."
    Who among us couldn't have used an astute resolute friend like Sonya during our worst teenage decisions? Hold the line, Sonya! MATT GALLAGHER

Everybody is worried about Natasha. I am too. But Andrei has been gone so long. He doesn't come to her. His letters are boring. What better way...
SHANNON STONEY

Who among you has never lusted after a scoundrel? MISS MAINWARING

My neighbor eloped back-in-the-day; my older sister helped her sneak out. I remember the thrill of it all, even the sounds. TERESA FINN

I'll say it: I want to fight Anatole. Which is as much a testament to Tolstoy's rich writing of character as it is to my own personal deficiencies. (Still, though. Flagpole, 3:00 P.M., Anatole. Be there.) MATT GALLAGHER

So everybody in *War and Peace* is forever restless and dives into unhappiness, which tells you that fucking things up for yourself is truly universal.
ANNIE LIONTAS

TODAY,
TOLSTOY TOGETHER
IS MIDWAY
THROUGH THE
JOURNEY OF
WAR AND PEACE.

YIYUN LI

She sobbed with that despair with which people weep only over a grief of which they feel themselves the cause.

Often we look outward for the causes of our grief, and find them where we look: the world never runs out of blameworthiness. It takes a rare and self-abandoning courage to acknowledge the most devastating kind of grief and say: I am its singular cause.

—

"Through Mlle Bourienne, Prince Nikolai Andreich knew all the rumors going around town"—including Anatole's attempted abduction of Natasha.

Mlle Bourienne has lived mostly in the country and is an outsider in Moscow. How does she know the rumors? (Is it possible she's kept in touch with Anatole? Or does she know a Frenchwoman in another house—a governess or a companion?)

—

If I were not I, but the handsomest, brightest, and best man in the world, and I was free, I would go on my knees this minute and ask for your hand and your love.

Pierre seems to be the only man in the novel capable of thinking *"If I were not I."* Others—Andrei, old Prince Bolkonsky, Rostov, Anatole—think "It must be so because I am who I am."

TRUE LOVE

Natasha is a hunted hare. Mother unavailable, useless father, no Nikolai, left to the dogs by Andrei. What makes a young woman lively and beautiful, makes her vulnerable—til she learns to protect herself. MISS MAINWARING

"As a wounded animal at bay looks at the approaching dogs and hunters, Natasha looked from one to the other." The shame and humiliation targeting Natasha after the botched abduction lulls us into a feeling of contempt—so potent we can't see her clearly—until this line reminds us she is seventeen, in a brutal world that eats its young (without admitting it). WAYNE SCOTT

> It reminds me of the line at the opera, when she returns to her father's box *"now totally subjected to the world she was in."* MEGAN CUMMINS

> I like this notion, Natasha as being subject to a corrupt world, better than mine, which was seeing Tolstoy depicting Natasha as shallow. LAWRENCE COATES

Andrei *"grinned coldly, spitefully, unpleasantly, like his father."* We swear we will not mirror our parents' faults, then the misfortunes of life hit us, and we understand what happened to them just as it happens to us. KIRTAN NAUTIYAL

> A marvelous range of emotion. The grin shifts with each adverb, until we see Andrei morphing into his father. LAURA SPENCE-ASH

Pierre gets the trifecta of Nabokov's definition of true love: *"And the feeling of pity, tenderness, and love took hold even more of Pierre."* THOMAS J. KITSON

Andrei and Pierre both undergo a transformative, sky-blessed love for Natasha, but whereas Andrei falls for her at her literal heights (in the rooms above him at Otradnoe), Pierre falls for her here at her depths. The contrast of idealizing versus pitying love. MOLLY ELIZABETH PORTER

It delights me to read of men in love bathing in moonlight and starshine to near ecstasy—both Pierre and Andrei—both in love with Natasha—or is it Natasha herself who taught them how to reach this state? JULIA AZAR RUBIN

VOLUME
THREE

YIYUN LI

START
Volume III,
Part One, I
"Since the
end of the
year 1811"

Fatalism in history is inevitable for the explanation of senseless phenomena (that is, those whose sense we do not understand). The more we try to explain sensibly these phenomena of history, the more senseless and incomprehensible they become for us.

END
Volume III,
Part One, V
"Alexander
had sent
him off."

It is unlikely that Tolstoy's time was sensible and comprehensible. Ours is not. Perhaps there is never a sensible and comprehensible time. Feeling fatalistic about history, though, is easier than feeling fatalistic about what has not yet become history.

—

Napoleon surveyed the river, dismounted, and sat on the log that lay on the bank. At a wordless sign he was handed a field glass, placed it on the back of a happy page who ran over, and began to look at the other side.

Napoleon, or Tolstoy's Napoleon, has the air of an actor too confident of his performance to realize that he has overacted.

—

As soon as the king began to speak loudly and quickly, all his kingly dignity instantly left him, and, not noticing it himself, he went over to his proper tone of good-natured familiarity.

Murat, a lesser actor, slips out of his role easily into his natural self.

THE PERFORMANCE OF WAR

After so much domestic drama, I am thrilled to be back in wartime, cackling away at Tolstoy's descriptions of these men and their games. SARA BETH WEST

The sovereign "*found a phrase which later became famous, which he liked himself, and which fully expressed his feelings.*" From those in command, the focus is on the words, the performance of war. LAURA SPENCE-ASH

My favorite part of the Briggs translation is he actually writes *"fuck"* where others use lighter words. It's war! Let them curse! KYLE FRANCIS WILLIAMS

I am having trouble focusing on their war. I can only think of the current world: Deranged leaders wreaking havoc. Reason no match for brute force and absurdity. Silliness of man games. History recycling. MISS MAINWARING

"There are two sides to the life of every man: the personal life which is free to the degree that its interests are abstract, and the life of the swarm in which one ineluctably follows the laws decreed for him." Tolstoy's characters—that is, we all—struggle with independence versus obligation. ANNIE LIONTAS

I'm captivated by the swimming Polish horsemen, grabbing one another, swept off their horses and disappearing into the current while Napoleon sits on the log, indifferent. It's a scene that made me want to write historical fiction. JOHN NEELEMAN

Making Balashev wait four days to see Napoleon has me grinning and wondering where my alliances lie. Lots of little humbling satisfying moments in *War and Peace*. MIKE PALINDROME

How small you make a man when you make him wait, as seen at the DMV and every government institution. ANNIE LIONTAS

Tolstoy would have loved this from Thoreau: "I called on the king, but he made me wait in his hall, and conducted like a man incapacitated for hospitality. There was a man in my neighborhood who lived in a hollow tree. His manners were truly regal. I should have done better had I called on him." ROBERT SULLIVAN

DAY 44
APRIL 30

START
Volume III,
Part One, VI
"Accustomed
though Balashov
was"

END
Volume III,
Part One, VIII
"presented them-
selves to Prince
Andrei one after
the other."

YIYUN LI

Directing his speech... at proving his rightness and his strength.

The whole aim of his speech now was obviously to exalt himself.

Napoleon was in that state of irritation in which a man has to talk and talk and talk, only so as to prove his rightness to himself.

Tolstoy foresees our miseries (and future generations'). Is there any solace in knowing that there is never a unique buffoon, a unique egotist, a unique sociopath, a unique dictator?

—

Mlle Bourienne was the same coquettish girl, pleased with herself, joyfully making use of every moment of her life.

Andrei is good at blaming all his father's follies on Mlle Bourienne, but *"making use of every moment"* seems a consistent and democratic approach to life—instead of his own approach of having one epiphany after another.

—

He was not thinking about this pretty boy, his son, as he held him on his lap, but about himself... Worst of all for him was that he sought and did not find in himself the former tenderness for his son.

This brings me back to the beginning of the novel, when the older women comment on the budding love between Sonya and Nikolai: The teenage lovers only have to deal with the uncertainty of young love, subject to a changeable heart. Parental love, less fickle, nevertheless banishes a child from a parent's thought more easily. A child, held on the lap of his loving parent, can slip into the role of a prop. Who are they to say that as your parents, they know even remotely who you are? They only know who they are to you.

ARMFELDT'S GRANDFATHER

"But no, he has preferred to surround himself with my enemies. And who precisely?... Armfeldt—a lecher and conspirator."

I wondered whether this was the same Swedish general named Armfeldt I learned about on a trip to Sweden. Turns out it wasn't, but his story resonates with events in 1812: Carl Gustav Armfeldt was the great-grandfather of the Armfeldt in *War and Peace*. He fought under Sweden's King Charles XII, who invaded Russia in 1714 and was defeated at the battle of Poltava, which Balachev refers to during his visit to Napoleon. In 1717 Charles ordered Armfeldt to attack the Norwegian city of Trondheim, hoping to defeat Sweden's enemies so he could invade Russia again. The attack failed, and Armfeldt was retreating when, on New Year's Eve, he learned Charles was dead.

Armfeldt's soldiers were known as Karoliners, after Charles's Latin name. When he invaded Norway in August he had 10,000 of them. Now, 6,000. Still, the situation on New Year's Day could have been worse. They were almost back to Sweden. The nearest friendly village was only two days' march away. The weather was cold but clear. Armfeldt's Karoliners were a mixture of locals and Finns, not soft Frenchmen from the sunny Mediterranean. But they were hungry, tired and poorly equipped, and when a fierce storm blew in, their guide, who knew the way back to Sweden, was among the first to die.

Armfeldt's army split. Half skirted the mountains, chopped a hole in an ice-covered river to find out which way it flowed, and followed it first to the village of Handöl and then to their supply base at Duved. By the time they reached it, 1,000 had perished. The other half of Armfeldt's army followed a faint track into the hills: a more direct route to safety, today dotted with emergency shelters and hostels supplying warm beds and expensive beer. But none of that existed in 1718. Caught in the icy wasteland of the Sylan massif, amid a howling gale, the Karoliners burned dwarf birch, heather, and their own rifle butts in a desperate effort to stay alive. To no avail: days later, pursuing Norwegian soldiers found thousands of frozen corpses. All told, Armfeldt lost 3,000 men. There's a monument to the "Carolean Death March" on the outskirts, and a commemorative trail marks their path. My favorite memorial, however, is at Norway's Trondheim University, where the first name on the sign-up list of student-run orienteering and mountain navigation courses is always the same: C. G. Armfeldt. Perhaps someone should do the same for Napoleon. **MARGARET HARRIS**

DAY 45
MAY 1

I DON'T KNOW WHAT THE CRITICS WILL SAY
TURGENEV AND FLAUBERT

START
Volume III,
Part One, IX
"Prince Andrei
arrived in
the general
headquarters"

END
Volume III,
Part One, XII
"'Here. What
lightning!' they
said to each
other."

Croisset
Friday 26 December 1879

Generous man,

I have not yet received the caviar or the salmon. By what means did you dispatch these two boxes? My stomach is ravaged with anxiety....

I am now preparing the last eight pages of my Religion. I am afraid that that chapter will be rather dry.

Your

G. FLAUBERT

50 rue de Douai Paris
Saturday morning, 27 December 1879

The caviar and salmon were sent *4 days* ago 'care of *M. Pilon,* quai du Havre, Rouen—to be handed to M. G.F.'... Find out what you can. I should be particularly sorry if the salmon were to be lost, it was splendid.

This cold spell is freezing me—and reducing me to stupidity. However I have started preparations for my departure. "The wine (what a wine!!) has been opened—it must be drunk."

I shall send you shortly a novel in 3 vols by Count Leo Tolstoy, whom I consider to be the foremost contemporary writer. You know who in my opinion could challenge him in that position. Unfortunately it has been translated by a Russian lady... and in general I am apprehensive about lady translators, especially when it's such a vigorous writer as Tolstoy is.

In the meantime, I embrace you. Your

I. T.

Croisset
Tuesday evening, 30 December 1879

Thank you! Many, many thanks, oh Saint Vincent de Paul of gastronomy! My word, you are treating me like a kept man! Too many deliciacies! Well I must tell you that I'm eating the caviar almost without bread, like jam.

As for the novel, its three volumes frighten me. Three volumes unconnected with my work are hard going now. Never mind, I shall tackle it....

When are you leaving, or rather when are you coming back? It's stupid to love one another as we do and to see so little of each other.

I embrace you. Your old

G. FLAUBERT

Croisset

Wednesday evening, 21 January 1880

Thank you for making me read Tolstoy's novel. It's first rate. What a painter and what a psychologist! The first two are sublime; but the third goes terribly to pieces. He repeats himself and he philosophises! In fact the man, the author, the Russian are visible, whereas up until then one had seen only Nature and Humanity. It seems to me that in places he has some elements of Shakespeare. I uttered cries of admiration during my reading of it... and it's long! Tell me about the *author*. Is it his first book? In any case he has his head *well screwed on!* Yes! It's very good! Very good!

I've finished my Religion and I'm working on the plan of my last chapter: Education. Your old

G. FLAUBERT

50 rue de Douai Paris

Saturday 24 January 1880

My good old fellow,

You cannot imagine the pleasure your letter gave me and what you say about Tolstoy's novel. Your approval confirms my own ideas about him. Yes, he is a man of great talent, and yet you put your finger on the weak spot: he also has built himself a philosophical system, which is at one and the same time mystical, childish and presumptuous, and which has spoilt his third volume dreadfully, and the second novel that he wrote after *War and Peace*—and where there are also things of the first order. I don't know what the critics will say (I have sent *War and Peace* to Daudet and Zola as well.) But for me the matter is settled: *Flaubert dixit*. The rest is of no significance.

I am pleased to see that your old fellows are coming along.

I'll be leaving Paris in the course of next week, but I'll write you a note before I go. In the meantime I embrace you. Your

IV. TURGENEV

YIYUN LI

START
Volume III,
Part One, XIII
"In a
abandoned
tavern"

END
Volume III,
Part One, XVIII
"And it seemed
to her that
God heard
her prayer."

A moment later Rostov's horse struck the officer's horse in the rump... almost knocking it down.

The selflessness of Tolstoy's animals: Rostov's horse does exactly what Uncle's dog Rugai has done—*"raced with a terrible self-lessness right onto the hare."*

—

It seemed so natural for Pierre to be kind to everyone, that there was no merit in his kindness.

Everyone else can stay in 1812. Pierre: Come this way, step into an Aesop fable.

—

Natasha's grief began to be covered over by the impressions of ongoing life, it ceased to weigh with such tormenting pain on her heart, it began to become the past, and Natasha started to recover physically.

"The impressions of ongoing life" is the amber that keeps grief secure inside.

A MASTER OF THE JUXTAPOSITION

Tolstoy's competing theses—history is inevitable and determined, even though the outcome of a battle hangs on whether a soldier shouts "we're lost!" or "hurrah!"—remind me of the divide between quantum mechanics and general relativity in physics. As in physics, the theory of the big (planets, stars, the grand sweep of history) is utterly incompatible with the theory of the small (atoms, electrons, individual actions). And yet our world—and *War and Peace*—sweeps on, serenely untroubled by the contradiction.
MARGARET HARRIS

Tolstoy is the master of the juxtaposition, whether it's a character, a chapter, or a line like, *"Everything began to glisten and sparkle. And with that light, as if in response to it, came the sound of guns ahead."* **ANNIE LIONTAS**

"Rostov couldn't take his mind off the brilliant exploit which, to his astonishment, had won him the St George's Cross and a heroic reputation. There was something odd about it. 'It turns out they're even more scared than we are,' he thought. 'Is this it then? Is this what they mean by heroism? Did I really do it for my country? And what has he done wrong with his dimple and his blue eyes? He was so scared! He thought I was going to kill him. Why should I want to kill him? My hand shook. And they've given me the George Cross! I can't see it, I just can't see it!'"
   To be humbly, honestly confused: something refreshing about Rostov's reaction to being honored for what he never did with honors in mind. I love a reluctant hero. **CARL PHILLIPS**

"Natasha walked... bearing herself as only a woman can, with poise and dignity totally belying the pain and shame of her heart."
   Yes, exactly. Isn't there a male equivalent, a way they hide their pain and shame? **HEATHER WOLF**

"Something stood sentinel within her and forbade her every joy."
   That's the most apt and succinct description of depression I've ever seen. **SARAH MEYER**

DAY 47
MAY 3

START
Volume III,
Part One, XIX
"Since the day
when Pierre,
leaving the
Rostovs'"

END
Volume III,
Part One, XXIII
"astonished
at what they
had done."

YIYUN LI

Petya was counting on the success of his undertaking precisely because he was a child... yet... he wanted to make himself look like an old man.

"Time travels in diverse paces with diverse persons." Still, one wishes the boy wouldn't rush so.

—

The Moscow hawkers remind me of Turgenev's observation about hot chocolate and cigar vendors in his letter to Pauline Viardot, written from the frontline during the Paris revolution:

> Greedy, pleased, and unconcerned, they had the look of fishermen hauling in a heavy laden net.

In every catastrophe there is a laden net.

—

For inspiration, a crowd needs to have a tangible object of love and a tangible object of hatred. Pierre had become the latter.

Hang in there, Pierre. Those characters who hate you in a brainless manner will love you in the same manner soon!

A COMPANION

If you could choose one character from *War and Peace* as your shelter-in-place buddy for this stressed moment of our *"elemental, swarmlike life,"* to be locked up with for the duration, who would it be, and why? WAYNE SCOTT

> After musing about this all night, I'm going to go with Hélène, not because the conversation would be so great, but because 1.) I want to see what makes her tick; 2.) I think the absence of anyone to attend her coif would break her down, reveal her true colors. WAYNE SCOTT

> Perhaps Tikhon? It would be helpful for the addled mental state: catch things when I angrily throw them, kiss my shoulder when I look upset. But maybe a servant isn't quite a buddy... MOLLY ELIZABETH PORTER

> Uncle. He knows how to live. MISS MAINWARING

> Andrei. He reminds me of a friend and mentor who also would have been described as stubborn and ridiculous, but with a heart of gold. All who knew him were driven bats by his idiosyncrasies and treasured him all the same. SALVADOR ORTEGA

> Andrei can only be loved as an idea and called upon as a God. ELOPE_

> No mention of Mademoiselle Bourienne? She is an experienced "companion," after all. MICHAEL G. FAULKNER

> Speransky! A well-read physicist—we would never run out of amazing things to talk about. SIGRID PAUEN

> But his hands! MISS MAINWARING

> Perhaps Marya—she has a level of awareness that is lacking in many of the other characters. We'd disagree on many things (e.g., religion), which would make for interesting conversations. ROBERT P. DROUIN

> Egad, quarantined with Marya?!! SALVADOR ORTEGA

YIYUN LI

START
Volume III,
Part Two, I
"Napoleon
started the
war with
Russia"

END
Volume III,
Part Two, IV
"he spurred
his horse and
rode down
the lane."

Tikhon walking old Prince Bolkonsky about in the house, looking for a place to sleep: Who among us has a loyal friend like Tikhon, who would, if sleeplessness were a bullet, take it, night after night.

—

The bell was tied up, and the harness bells were stopped with bits of paper. The prince did not allow anyone in Bald Hills to drive with bells. But Alpatych liked bells on a long journey.

Bald Hills is forty miles east of Smolensk. It comforts one to think of Alpatych listening to the bells on that white night, summer of 1812, for forty drowsy and peaceful miles, before the cannonballs fall near him in Smolensk.

During one of the most historical moments in the novel, Tolstoy once again draws the readers' attention to the terminable and interminable moments in each individual's life.

—

Done for! Russia! I'll set the fire myself!

The fire in Smolensk, a prelude to the Fire of Moscow, starts right next to Alpatych—who bears witness for what's missed by the tsar and his courtiers, Rostov and his fellow officers, Pierre and Moscow society.

NO CIRCUMSTANCE IS SO DIRE
THAT BERG CAN'T MAKE IT SEEM ABSURD

Alphonse Karlovych Berg is the not-so-great pretender of *War and Peace*. *"The son of an obscure Livonian nobleman,"* Berg rises through the ranks of the Russian Army not by doing great things on the battlefield but by mimicking his superiors and blindly following the rules even when the rules no longer make sense. After marrying Vera, the buzz-killing oldest daughter of the Rostovs, Berg advises her, *"You can imitate something, you can ask for something."* Thus he wears his side whiskers as the Emperor Alexander does; his carriage and gray horses are *"exactly like those of a certain prince"*; he takes leave to go to Moscow, though he has nothing to do there, because everyone in the army takes leave to go to Moscow; and, best of all, he considers an acquaintance a friend *"only because he knew that all people had friends."*

There's a strange incomprehension to Berg, an empty space that he fills with covetous and optimistic calculation. A week before his wedding to Vera, he informs the cash-strapped Count Rostov that he will call off the marriage unless given a dowry of thirty thousand in cash (they settle on twenty thousand plus a promissory note). Four hundred pages later, during the chaotic evacuation of Moscow, Berg exhausts even the count's patience by asking for the loan of a muzhik to help him make off with some abandoned furniture, explaining that it's really for Verushka. No one seems persuaded by Berg's imitation of greatness, but they find something disarming in his *"naïve and good-natured egoism."*

Like most of us, he can't help being who he is, and I welcome his rare and carefully timed appearances. Take the brief encounter between Berg and Prince Andrei on the night Smolensk falls to Napoleon's forces. As the people burn their city to delay the French advance, Andrei dispatches a message to his sister, Princess Marya, directing her to flee the family estate forty miles away. Into this scene arrives Berg on horseback, now with the lengthy title of *"assistant to the chief of staff of the left flank of the infantry of the first army."* He sizes up the situation, badly, and, not realizing who he's talking to, berates Andrei, threatening to make him pay for doing nothing to stop the burning. Reading this, I expect that someone is finally going to tell Berg where to get off, but the prince is much cooler than that: *"Prince Andrei looked at him and, without replying, went on addressing Alpatych."* It's a silent dis for the ages, yet I imagine that Berg, being Berg, will not be troubled by it for very long. TOM DRURY

DAY 49
MAY 5

YIYUN LI

START
Volume III,
Part Two, V
"From Smolensk
the troops
continued to
retreat."

END
Volume III,
Part Two, VII
"He gave
Lavrushka
another horse
and took him
along."

Two girls , their skirts filled with plums picked from the conservatory trees, ran out from there and met Prince Andrei.... Prince Andrei turned away from them in frightened haste, afraid of letting them notice that he had seen them.... A new, comforting, and reassuring feeling came over him when, looking at these girls, he realized the existence of other human interests, totally foreign to him and as legitimate as those that concerned him.

Sometimes a man sees better once he learns how not to be seen.

—

The old man still sat as indifferently as a fly on the face of a dead loved one.

Strange that Andrei sees the plum-stealing girls for the first time as real human beings, yet the old peasant, who sits on the old prince's bench, is still seen as a fly.

—

All that naked, white human flesh... was flopping about in the dirty puddle like carp in a bucket. This flopping about suggested merriment, and that made it particularly sad.

Andrei is flopping too. So are most of us. The unflopping ones we cannot trust.

HOW TO SUCCEED

"A good player who loses at chess is genuinely convinced that he has lost because of a mistake, and he looks for this mistake in the beginning of his game, but forgets that there are also mistakes at every step in the course of the game, that none of his moves was perfect. The mistake he pays attention to is conspicuous only because his opponent took advantage of it." In the future, I may have my Little League teams read *War and Peace*.
BOB HILLMAN

"A good commander not only does not need genius or any special qualities, but, on the contrary, he needs the absence of the best and highest qualities—love, poetry, tenderness, a searching philosophical doubt."
  Tolstoy, on why we are doomed. GARTH GREENWELL

When I was in college, there was a leadership class in the business school with *War and Peace* as the primary text. I didn't take it, since I opposed anything practical, but now I wonder how the discussion would have gone.
BOB HILLMAN

"The small, muddy green pond had evidently risen some eight inches, overflowing the dam, because it was filled with the naked human bodies of soldiers flopping about in it."
  This seems impossibly great to me—it makes the whole world unimpeachably real and alive. GARTH GREENWELL

Quite an achievement to describe a retreating army and leave the reader primarily with the stifling impression of a stagnant, oppressive, breezeless August day. THOMAS J. KITSON

Counted at least seven mentions of spurs to date. Today Andrei puts them to his horse. Remember Denisov dancing in them? MISS MAINWARING

Celebrating Cinco de Mayo, a victory over another Napoleon at the Battle of Puebla. ZULMA ORTIZ-FUENTES

DAY 50
MAY 6

START
Volume III,
Part Two, VIII
"Princess Marya
was not
in Moscow"

END
Volume III,
Part Two, X
"she was
ready to do
everything
for him and for
the muzhiks."

YIYUN LI

I wished for his death. Yes, I wished it would end sooner... I wanted to be at peace... But what will become of me? What do I need peace for, if he won't be there?

Her father's death brings Princess Marya to her most humane moment: religion, of little use, has retreated.

—

With the same smile of agreement with which it had been his habit over fifteen years to respond, without expressing his own opinions...

One suspects that the architect Mikhail Ivanovich is only waiting to go into a William Trevor story and surprise us all.

—

"I see through everything seven feet under you" is such an effective threat. I too looked down at the floor underneath me with dread when I read the sentence.

THANK YOU... FORGIVE ME

Old Prince Andrei losing his wits is terrifying for Marya, whose entire world has been built around him, so much so that she *"is even afraid to think of it"* and turns pale hearing about his degradation. But it also makes her curious about the world. ANNIE LIONTAS

I am hopeful for Marya. ELEONORE

I worry her curiosity has come too late. ANSER

I'm at the periphery with a cowbell and swag—hoping she can "go the distance." TERESA FINN

"I want him to die."
Crazy but I found this moving. *"The spiritual world where she had been incarcerated."* The talk of temptation by devils. Her slumbered hopes of love and life awakened. MIKE PALINDROME

Prince Bolkonsky was a cruel, embittered old man, and yet Tolstoy gives him perfect final words for anyone at the end of a complicated relationship: *"Forgive me... Thank you... Forgive me... Thank you."* JEFFREY MORRIS

Marya, tormented with sadness as guilt: William Trevor wrote, "to be sad is rather like to be guilty... people should feel guilty sometimes... I think it can be something that really renews people." ELEONORE

Irish guilt. It is heavy and useful. TERESA FINN

So relieved Marya is finally freed from her father's tyranny. SIEL JU

Mlle Bourienne is wearing weepers (known in French as *"pleureuses"*). These are part of mourning dress: a strip of white linen or muslin worn on the cuff of a sleeve, used to wipe one's eyes/nose when weeping. They were worn by both men and women. MICHAEL G. FAULKNER

Imagine having the time—and the consent of society—to mourn, and to mourn publicly. MICHAEL C. RUSH

DAY 51
MAY 7

YIYUN LI

START
Volume III,
Part Two, XI
"An hour later
Dunyasha
came to
the princess"

END
Volume III,
Part Two, XV
"'Oh, German
scrupulosity!'
he said,
shaking his
head."

She kept thinking about one thing—her grief, which, after the interruption caused by the cares of the present, had already become her past.

Few things are as consistent as time's indifference. The interruptions of today will become the past, too.

—

At their meeting neither Princess Marya nor Rostov mentions Natasha and Andrei and their broken engagement. For that alone they have already what makes a good couple: some things are better kept unsaid.

—

He despised them not with his intelligence, or feeling, or knowledge... He despised them with his old age, with his experience of life.

I wonder which is preferable: to have that experience of life, or to be rather the target of such contempt.

THE FACES OF THE CROWD

"'What, us abandon everything? We don't agree. We don't agree... We're sorry for you, but we're not in agreement. You go by yourself...' came from different sides of the crowd. And again one and the same expression appeared on all the faces of the crowd, and now it was certainly not an expression of curiosity and gratitude, but of angry resolve."

Their world devastated, danger on the horizon, misinformation rampant, the crowd of peasants devolves into anger, distrust, dissension. How do we deal with change on this scale? What is the "real truth"? **WAYNE SCOTT**

Serfdom is abhorrent. And yet, I found myself cheering on Nikolai as he put those treacherous peasants in their place and rescued Marya. What is wrong with me? **LAWRENCE COATES**

Thinking of the small and failed revolutions that are forgotten, made up of "boorish" people, ending with the prevailing of status quo. I felt the pain and embarrassment when Dron, the village elder, took off his own belt to bind himself. **YVONNE YEVAN YU**

"Rostov immediately imagined something romantic in the encounter."

Nikolai is once again sensitive to the literariness of the scene and knows the role he ought to be playing. This time, it comes off almost perfectly and without regret. That's an aspect of Nikolai's character that surprised me this time around. I remember him as that cutting *"mediocre."* **THOMAS J. KITSON**

"She could not be blamed if for the rest of her life, without ever speaking of it to anyone, she continued to love the man she had fallen in love with for the first and last time."

Characters drop like flies for love in *War and Peace*. **ANNIE LIONTAS**

All of the love that's spoken in *War and Peace* is in French, and all unspoken, in Russian. **ANNIE LIONTAS**

"Spoken words are silver, unspoken words are gold."

We're *constantly* reminded of the physicality of Pierre, Napoleon, Hélène, but then radio silence on Andrei's body. He's just vaguely handsome and medium height with no descriptors, almost a ghostlike figure with no corporeal existence. MOLLY ELIZABETH PORTER

What did you think about Kutuzov's hug? His body is always emphasized (getting fatter like Pierre) and here, he swallows Andrei in his embrace and *"didn't let him go for a long time."* THOMAS J. KITSON

All the characters are gaining weight as war gets closer. WAYNE SCOTT

The embrace was so striking. Andrei's a character I'm never quite sure where to place. The more I think about him the more I feel there's a fundamental unknowability about him, in spite of (because of?) how much we're in his head. Kind of like *Anna Karenina*—I always link Andrei and Anna together for some reason, even though they have very different lives. MOLLY ELIZABETH PORTER

He often feels so cold, whereas many of us are immediately drawn to Pierre, who has a ton of really objectionable flaws. The Anna connection: Maybe we're facing a question about judging others—as Marya tries so hard to avoid. We feel like we know Pierre and we overlook (forgive) almost without thinking. Andrei, oddly enough, invites some of our harshest judgments. THOMAS J. KITSON

"She saw him before her with the expression he had had in the coffin, on his face bound with a white handkerchief."
How often the color white is used here, with great effect. It stands out in relief against the rich and swirling narrative. LAURA SPENCE-ASH

"Prince Andrei knew Denisov from Natasha's stories about her first suitor. That memory now carried him back sweetly and painfully to those aching feelings which he had not thought of for a long time now, but which were still there in his soul."

The return of Denisov is the best thing that happened to me today. MISS MAINWARING

"How many years have you been feeding off the community?" Karp yelled at him. "It's all the same to you! You'll dig up your money box and take it with you, so what's it to you if our houses are devastated."

DAY 52
MAY 8

YIYUN LI

START
Volume III,
Part Two, XVI
"'Well, that's
all now!' said
Kutuzov"

END
Volume III,
Part Two, XIX
"three hours
from total
destruction
and flight."

There's no need to storm and attack, there's need for patience and time.

"Patience and time": three simple and enduring words from a novel of more than half a million words.

—

The princess was clearly annoyed that there was no one to be angry with.

Not even with herself? It must be a strange kind of helplessness to have no one to be angry with.

—

Tolstoy on history—I like to imagine one of my favorite Rebecca West characters cutting off his musings and consoling him:

> The world is a preposterous place. It is very brave of us to teach history in schools, it is so discouraging.

THE ANCIENTS

"The ancients left us examples of heroic poems in which heroes constitute the entire interest of history, and we still cannot get used to the fact that, for our human time, history of this sort has no meaning."
Tolstoy is rarely more modern than that! JEFFREY MORRIS

Or as Tina Turner would say, "We don't need another hero." ROBERT DEAM TOBIN

Our tether to the far past, an endless fascination. JOHN NEELEMAN

The individual versus history. The Muscovites party, which seems bad; Kutuzov calmly watches history unfold, which seems good; Pierre leaves things up to the cards. ROBERT DEAM TOBIN

Borodino, the bloodiest battle ever at that point in history. Kutuzov brought a French novel to read to it. Lermontov wrote a poem about it. I almost bought an incredibly hard-to-play board game about it. MIKE PALINDROME

Tolstoy spent two days in September 1867 studying the battlefield of Borodino and comparing the terrain with historical accounts of the battle, after which he sketched a map correcting the description of the historians. PEVEAR AND VOLOKHONKSY

This biographical footnote soothed me while following the painfully detailed battle scenario, and reminded me of Melville's obsessive chapter on the whale in *Moby-Dick*. GENEVIEVE WOLLENBECKER

To write a great novel, one must be obsessed, even if crankily, like Ahab with Moby-Dick, his nemesis that, in life, was "only" a creature, not a fate. Ahab's crazed obsession equals Melville's obsession to create the great epic tragedy of human life, as he envisioned it. JOYCE CAROL OATES

"He had in his hand a French book which he closed as Prince Andrew entered, marking the place with a knife."
I was on Kutuzov's side until exactly this sentence. ADAM SNYDER

DAY 53
MAY 9

START
Volume III,
Part Two, XX
"On the
morning of the
twenty-fifth"

END
Volume III,
Part Two, XXIV
"'They'd gone
to the estate
outside
Moscow.'"

YIYUN LI

Twenty thousand of them are doomed to die, yet they get surprised at my hat!

Oh dear Pierre: it's your hat today, not the twenty thousand deaths tomorrow, that makes this moment real.

—

One might think of how many would be missing the next day, but one ought not to speak of it.

Yes, the world would be a grippingly bleak place if all people spoke aloud their thoughts uncensored.

—

"On this living terrain he could not find a position and could not even distinguish our troops from the enemy's."

I was happy to learn from Edmund White that Tolstoy's rendition of wartime confusions was influenced by Stendhal, who wrote about the confusion at Waterloo in his novel *The Charterhouse of Parma*.

Stendhal—entrusted with a portfolio of letters from Marie Louise to her husband, Napoleon—traveled to Moscow in 1812. There, he rescued a beautiful edition of Voltaire from the fire, meaning to take it home as a souvenir, and then had to flee with his compatriots.

Stefan Zweig and V. S. Pritchett both wrote wonderfully about Stendhal's time in Moscow (as well as his life as a writer).

> Stendhal hardly has time to save himself with his wonted care (and he is the only officer in the Grand Amy to trouble to do such a thing under the peculiar circumstances of the retreat!) before he is obliged to scurry across the bridge if he is not

to be submerged with its ruins. His diary, his Historie de la peinture, his beautiful edition of Voltaire, his horse, his fine new furs, his valise—all are left behind for the Cossacks to enjoy. With torn clothes, dirty, hunted, bedraggled, his hands and face chapped by exposure to the frosty air, he makes good his escape to Prussia. A gasp of relief—and forthwith he goes to the opera. **STEFAN ZWEIG**

When the great fire starts he seems to keep his head and to display sang-froid—or so people reported. He was unconsciously collecting the material for the superb Waterloo chapter in *La Chartreuse de Parme*, and one catches its accent. (He was not at Waterloo.) **V. S. PRITCHETT**

We are constantly learning, consciously or unconsciously, while we read or talk with others. I was convinced that Stendhal had been *at* Waterloo, but he was only learning how to write about Waterloo by experiencing 1812 in Russia. We are, of course, also learning about our own time.

Writing during World War II, V. S. Pritchett commented on another book set around the same time: "One reads all books on the Napoleonic period with one eye continually jumping forward to the present."

We may as well take the leap and say: One reads with one eye continually jumping forward to the unknown.

DAY 54
MAY 10

START
Volume III,
Part Two, XXV
"The officers
wanted to take
their leave"

END
Volume III,
Part Two, XXVIII
"worthily
fulfilled his
role of
seeming to
command."

YIYUN LI

Pierre looked at Timokhin with the condescendingly question-
ing smile with which everyone involuntarily addressed him.

How I adore Timokhin: without fail, he gives people the opportunity to feel good about themselves. Even Pierre is not immune.

—

When Napoleon came out of the tent, the cries of the guards
before his son's portrait became louder still.... "Take him
away," he said, pointing to the portrait with a gracefully majes-
tic gesture. "It is still too early for him to look upon a field of
battle."

It must be tiresome to live for posterity. Other than winning
wars, Napoleon has also to think about winning readers of
history.

—

Along with a portfolio of letters for her husband, Napoleon's
empress also entrusted a portrait of their son to Henri Beyle
(later known as Stendhal) when he traveled to Moscow.

ESSENTIAL WORKERS

Today's reading is a perfect example of Tolstoy extolling the "instinctive 'truth' of the common people." (Andrzej Walicki) **ELLIOTT HOLT**

> And also a reaction to individualism (as supposedly embodied by Napoleon)? **KATHARINE HOLT**

We, along with Russian aristocrats, are gradually discovering the peasantry. Our first encounter, with Marya, was a little rough; now, with Pierre, we start to see how that "wildness" has a mysterious solidity to it. **THOMAS J. KITSON**

And Pierre, like so many recently, has a "sudden" epiphany about the value of essential workers. **STEPHANIE "ABBI" FLETCHER**

When Tolstoy proves the disposition of Napoleon incorrect point by point, it's less about the man or the battle and more about stories and their tellings and who gets to do the telling and the fluidity of truth. **SARA BETH WEST**

> Tolstoy's case against Napoleon—it's impossible not to notice a competition of wills. Tolstoy's own formidable ego, cloaked in his theory of history—his insistence that he is right. **WAYNE SCOTT**

"Having sat for a while and touched with his hand, not knowing why himself, the roughness of a highlight on the portrait..."
Tolstoy complicates characters with the smallest of details—here, a surprisingly quiet and sensuous moment for Napoleon. **LAURA SPENCE-ASH**

Tolstoy using Prince Andrei as his mouthpiece today, to express Tolstoy's personal views on war. Yet among that, I found the comments regarding the valet touching: better to be cared for clumsily but lovingly than to be cared for competently but clinically. **MICHAEL G. FAULKNER**

DAY 55
MAY 11

START
Volume III,
Part Two, XXIX
"Having returned
from a second
preoccupied
ride"

END
Volume III,
Part Two, XXXII
"a straining
man crying
out with his
last strength."

YIYUN LI

He did not want to sleep, the punch was finished, and there was still nothing to do.

Such listlessness. At 4:00 A.M., without his audience, even Napoleon cannot find something to sustain his ego.

—

A young, round-faced little officer, still a perfect child... said "Ah" and, curling up, sat on the ground like a bird shot down in flight.

Children lost on the battlefield remind one of infants falling into sudden sleep in the middle of a crying bout.

—

Both were perplexed about what they had done and what they were to do. "Am I taken prisoner, or have I taken him prisoner?" each of them thought.

Sometimes I ask the same question, not in combat with an enemy, but in my wrestling with writing.

HERO JOURNEYS

The sense of family and camaraderie at the battle scene reminded me of a letter my father wrote home in December 1944, from somewhere in France, retyped by my grandfather:

> We have been under shelling for occasional but infrequent periods and perhaps the worst part of that is waiting for the next one to land. That is where the German technique of wearing down the nerves is most effective. But we have an overwhelming advantage in artillery—better than 5:1 and several times our guns have knocked out a German position before more than 4 shells came over. The sense of team work is never so strong as it is over here and when you hear your own guns behind you, arching over your head, and can hear your tanks and planes going out in front, you realize the war is the ultimate in many things and you're sorry that it takes such a chaos to bring out the extremes in the human being.
> **LAURA SPENCE-ASH**

Pierre, Andrei, Napoleon, and Nikolai seem like heroes in four competing genres—comedy, tragedy, epic, and romance (or maybe they just interpret their own lives this way)... all awkwardly, fascinatingly clashing. Pierre seems like he left his genre—stumbled onto the wrong stage—in today's reading (though I don't know if he's ever comfortably fit anywhere). This could maybe be extended to Berg and Vera as satire, Marya as hagiography, Natasha as lyric poetry. **MOLLY ELIZABETH PORTER**

> A fascinating way to think about the novel. I hear echoes of Northrop Frye, which is music to my ears; *Anatomy of Criticism* came to mind— the idea of different hero journeys and power fields. I love your idea that one novel can contain all the different heroes. I've never imagined such a beast. **MISS MAINWARING**

"This disposition, drawn up quite vaguely and confusedly—if one allows oneself to consider Napoleon's instructions without religious awe of his genius..." Tolstoy, after projecting authority, reveals that he himself is confused, and the confused reader smiles. **JOHN NEELEMAN**

DAY 56
MAY 12

YIYUN LI

START
Volume III,
Part Two, XXXIII
"The main
action of
the battle of
Borodino"

END
Volume III,
Part Two, XXXV
"vacillating
men were
comforted and
reassured."

In battle it is a matter of what is dearest to a man—his own life—and it sometimes seems that salvation lies in running back, sometimes in running forward.

Literature (and life) would be so boring if that word *"seems"* didn't exist.

—

If you see so poorly, my dear sir, don't allow yourself to speak of what you don't know.

Alas. To see poorly and to speak of what one doesn't know are only human. Is there one person who has not erred thus?

—

In undecided affairs it is always the most stubborn one who remains victorious.

Someday I would love to write an essay in praise of this pair of underrated virtues: stubbornness and indecisiveness.

BUT IT'S ALL TRUE

This entry from Tolstoy's 1906 diaries perhaps sheds light on Andrei's and Pierre's missing mothers:

> 10 March. Was in a dull, miserable state all day. By evening this state changed to one of emotion—the desire for affection—for love. I felt, as in childhood, like clinging to a loving, pitying creature, and weeping emotionally and being comforted. But who is the creature I could cling to like that? I ran through all the people I love—nobody would do. Who could I cling to? I wanted to become young again and cling to my mother as I imagine her to have been. Yes, yes, my dear mother whom I never called by that name, since I couldn't talk. Yes, she is my highest conception of pure love—not a cold or divine, but a warm, earthly, maternal love. This is what attracts my better, weary soul. Mother dear, caress me. All this is stupid, but it's all true.

I love the cynical sentimentality of "All this is stupid, but it's all true." It feels like a great opening line to a novel, like "All this happened, more or less." MOLLY ELIZABETH PORTER

> A key. Thank you. The only good mother in *War and Peace* is Mother Russia. MISS MAINWARING

> Remember the sweet moments Natasha had in bed with her mother? BERRY HOAK

> Perhaps there are two competing conceptions of Russia—as father, as mother—in *War and Peace*. The patriarchal, militaristic fatherland embodied by Andrei's father is being killed off and exposed in transition to the feminine Russian soul of Natasha. One conception of the Russian spirit is dying in favor of a gentler one, war to peace. The old order changeth, yielding to the new. MOLLY ELIZABETH PORTER

> I have been getting too annoyed with father and son, I should go back and read their sections with a bit more empathy. HARISH

DAY 57
MAY 13

YIYUN LI

START
Volume III,
Part Two, XXXVI
"Prince Andrei's
regiment
was in the
reserves"

END
Volume III,
Part Two, XXXIX
"the hand of
an adversary
stronger in
spirit."

A little brown dog with a stiffly raised tail, who, coming from God knows where, trotted out in front of the ranks with a preoccupied air.

Death is coming for him, too. Only, unlike the soldiers, the dog doesn't know it.

—

The horse... not asking whether it was good or bad to show fear, snorted, reared up.... The horse's terror communicated itself to the men.

Neither does the horse ask which is the politically and morally correct language to speak, French or Russian.

—

The horses were eating oats from their nosebags, and sparrows flew down to them, pecking up the spilled grain. Crows, scenting blood, crowing impatiently, flew about in the birches.

The animals live through war and peace with the same concern: to not starve.

But the greatest
attention was accorded
to totally extraneous
events, which had no
relation to battle. It was
as if the attention of
these morally exhausted
men found rest in these
ordinary everyday
events.

VOLUME III. TWO. XXXVI.

TO MAKE SPACE FOR WONDER

When I signed on to read *War and Peace* in installments of roughly ten to fifteen pages a day, I figured it was a reading method designed to make the monumental manageable—a distraction from the intimidation of 1,000+ pages, an encouragement to look at the immediate small task rather than at the larger, more Herculean labor. And it was definitely that. But only maybe halfway through the group reading did I realize I was learning not just a new way to read but a new way to see and, by extension, a new way to understand the world around me. I could look at the larger challenge of a pandemic that had been the catalyst for the reading group to begin with, or I could look at the smaller invitation of each day with its mix of responsibilities and pleasures. Sure, this is maybe just another version of taking each day at a time, but I have never found that advice irrelevant, and I definitely needed to be reminded of it, as the world began its rapid decline into a chaos (on so many levels) unlike any that I've known in my life.

What this meant, with respect to *War and Peace,* was that I started looking more closely at details I'd have passed over without thinking too much about them, had I been trying to read 100 pages a day. In particular, I started noticing how often Tolstoy will have a seemingly random animal appear in a scene. At one point, a dog appears at the roadside as an army is making its way from one town to the next, for example; some of the soldiers notice the dog, laugh or smile, variously, and move on. Why include this, I wondered, except for just something to include? Is this why the book was so long? Why not stick to the subjects of war and peace?

I think that, besides wanting to remind us of how our daily lives contain so many things that have no specific "meaning," Tolstoy is also suggesting that there are other dichotomies in our lives, and that these aren't at all irrelevant to the larger one of war and peace, but in fact are smaller manifestations of that dichotomy. In this juxtaposition of dog and army I see the obvious dichotomy of animal and human, but that quickly leads me to think about how dogs in particular have been domesticated by humans, and isn't domestication a version of war against wildness, a way of making the wild peaceful? So, the appearance of the dog in this scene resonates with and reinforces Tolstoy's governing theme.

Dogs also differ from humans in not being simultaneously gifted with and burdened by self-consciousness which, among its benefits, is what allows us to deliberate over a subject, to bring order to chaos, intellectually; it's also responsible for a lot of anxiety at times. A dog doesn't have the ability to think, for example, about whether or not today will be its last day on earth. On the other hand, a dog can't make a reasoned reflection about the past and use it as a way to navigate the future, of which a dog is unaware, as far as I know. For me, consciousness is a constant warring of many, often conflicting ideas, as the mind brings order to them, followed by a temporary calmness of mind, stability of thought. Peace. The presence of the dog in Tolstoy's scene doesn't overtly speak to this, but for me it was a catalyst—thanks to self-consciousness!—for thinking about dogs vis-à-vis human beings, the differences between us.

Also: what we share. For there are many shared areas between animals and humans. Tolstoy's dog, because of not having self-consciousness, also has an innocence to it, recalling an innocence that we're all born with, but which tends to fall into the shadows of experience as we grow up and into the world. In the scene I'm thinking of, the dog brings a smile and some laughter to the soldiers—for a moment, they're boys again. And for a moment I remember that even as adults we still carry inside us the children we were, those experiences don't go away, and even the ones we don't remember are still having their effects on how we proceed through our lives. Also, despite our prioritizing experience over innocence, we do still experience innocence and wonder as adults, more often as the result of an encounter with something more innocent—a child, an animal.

I've always tried to remind myself to find some joy, even just a small one, in each day. With the onset of the pandemic, I began deliberately making it more of a daily practice to make space for wonder, to remind myself: this, too, exists. I start most of my days by making a list of goals—chores, really, things I have to do, deadlines to meet, etc. That's part of the world of experience. Of being an adult. But since March, I've made more of a point to include on that list something as simple as "sit on the porch, close your eyes, and listen—what bird is singing that particular handful of notes?" Or, for another example, "lie down on the floor with your dog, breathe beside him, without thinking about it." For me, that's innocence. Remembering that has been a way to survive. I had to be reminded of the small details that get overlooked. Maybe we all need that reminder, fairly routinely. A random dog in a small scene in a very big book sparked my thinking. Who imagined reading *War and Peace* would be a way to get there? CARL PHILLIPS

DAY 58
MAY 14

YIYUN LI

START
Volume III,
Part Three, I
"For human
reason, absolute
continuity"

END
Volume III,
Part Three, V
"enormous
current of
people which
carried him
along with it."

A commander in chief always finds himself in the middle of a shifting series of events, and in such a way that he is never able at any moment to ponder all the meaning of the ongoing event.

The same for us, as the commanders in chief of our own chaotic lives.

—

Malasha also looked at Grandpa. She was closest to him of all and saw how his face winced; it was as if he was about to cry.

Only a child recognizes the helplessness in Kutuzov's unshed tears.

—

After that, the generals began to disperse with the same solemn and silent discretion as people dispersing after a funeral.

Bilibin: Where art thou?

HOW GRAND LIFE CAN BE

War and Peace reminds me of how grand life can be even when it appears so small, what it is to be human and that we're just little ants on this planet. At the same time, each of us ants can embody a whole universe of meaning in our own selves. **TATIANA**

These opening chapters of part three can be read as an argument for the novel, with its ability to inhabit the perspectives of many characters and to let action unfold in scenes versus history, which, in Tolstoy's view, is always reductive.

"*Only by admitting an infinitesimal unit for observation—a differential of history, that is, the uniform strivings of people—and attaining to the art of integrating them... can we hope to comprehend the laws of history.*" Hence this huge novel with many characters.

"*A commander in chief always finds himself in the middle of a shifting series of events, and in such a way that he is never able at any moment to ponder all the meaning of the ongoing event.*" Hence fictional scenes, which let us see men reacting in the moment. **ELLIOTT HOLT**

I feel like Schrödinger's cat during Tolstoy's historiographical bits, simultaneously alive to the thrilling scope of his ideas, and bored to death. **SARAH MEYER**

Oh God... after 751 pages and a grueling twenty-chapter battle scene—math. **RICHARD L. GORELICK**

In the midst of an essay on the infinitesimal math that drives history—impossible for humans to grasp as they grapple with what to do—six-year-old Malasha's nuanced view of what's happening (men angry at "Grandpa") is closer to the truth than anyone could realize. **WAYNE SCOTT**

"*Malasha, who looked at what was happening before her without taking her eyes away, understood the meaning of this council differently.*"
I love how Tolstoy provides us with the POV of a six-year-old, literally a bird's-eye view, as she sits atop the stove. **LAURA SPENCE-ASH**

Learning all kinds of tricks from Tolstoy, including if you're going to talk battle strategy, throw a kid on the stovetop and watch "Grandad versus Longcoat" go at it through Malasha's eyes. **ANNIE LIONTAS**

DAY 59
MAY 15

YIYUN LI

START
Volume III,
Part Three, VI
"Hélène, having
returned with
the court"

END
Volume III,
Part Three, XI
"saw any
more of
Pierre or
knew where
he was."

Princess Kuragin, *"constantly tormented by envy of her daughter,"* bemoans: *"How is it we didn't know it in our long-lost youth?"*

The apex of Hélène's success: she makes her mother envy her and regret not having left her father.

—

He handed Pierre a wooden spoon, after licking it clean.

A line that always makes me shiver with joy.

—

An ax would be a good thing, a spear wouldn't be bad, but a pitch-fork would be best: a Frenchman is no heavier than a sheaf of rye.

The difference between propaganda and comedy is that the author of the former doesn't laugh at his own creation.

WHAT YOU HAVE TO DO

Pierre goes to battle once and immediately gets Dear John'ed by Princess Hélène. Some war traditions really are instilled in the human condition! **MATT GALLAGHER**

I want to hear Hélène's side of the story: her dashed hopes at inheriting the old count's wealth, her marriage to the rich but socially impossible Pierre, her glittering social life, her many young admirers. **ROBERT DEAM TOBIN**

"Votre amie Hélène." Not! Tolstoy gives us the diplomatic machinations of a femme fatale also known as "La belle dame sans merci." **SIGRID PAUEN**

Suddenly developing a lot of respect and envy for Hélène—the woman knows how to get what she wants! **SIEL JU**

Something vaguely satisfying about *War and Peace*: The characters invariably receive from their creator a kind of rough (in both senses) justice. The discerning and charitable reader must be increasingly dreading what is in store for Hélène. **JOHN NEELEMAN**

This isn't highbrow book analysis at all, but Tolstoy's enduring, vast contempt for stupid, intellectually incurious people—in particular the Kuragins—is one of my favorite parts of this grand book. **MATT GALLAGHER**

> But isn't this also a matter of narrative perspective? I think the Rostovs are stupid, intellectually incurious people too, but we get the inner thoughts of Natasha and Nikolai and so relate to them, but we never get inside Hélène's or Anatole's heads. **HARISH**

"No, not unity. You can't unite your thoughts, you can harness thoughts, all of them together. Yes, that's what you have to do."
New favorite moment—Pierre/Pyotr, getting the secret of the existence, only to wake up and discover it's his groom, telling him it's time to hitch the horses. **BRIAN OLSON**

Not gonna lie, been walking around saying, *"They shall eat horseflesh yet."* **ANNIE LIONTAS**

DAY 60
MAY 16

START
Volume III,
Part Three, XII
"The Rostovs
remained in
the city"

END
Volume III,
Part Three, XVI
"tried to
take along
as much as
possible."

YIYUN LI

She could not and did not know how to do things if not with all her heart, with all her might.

One of the best traits: I see it in my favorite people, and I see it every day in our dog, too.

—

Moscow's last day came.

I wonder which other city in history also lives up to this solemn line. Pompei? Paris?

—

Berg bargaining for furniture and Sonia packing and unpacking and storing things: they both, in their own way, provide relief in this tumultuous time.

BOTH EYES OPEN

Tolstoy shows that the self-help book is a redundancy: *"They laughed and were gay, not in the least because there was reason for laughter. But they were gay and glad at heart, and so everything that happened was reason enough for gaiety and laughter in them."* ROBERT P. DROUIN

From the chaos of the battlefield to the chaos of the Rostov household, where women reign and Natasha and Sonya lead the domestic troops. ZULMA ORTIZ-FUENTES

I've been pondering the "Which character do you most identify with" question. With the chapters on packing up the Rostovs' house, I have realized, with a heavy heart, that it is Sonya. MARGARET HARRIS

> Why a heavy heart? Sonya and Marya are my two favorite characters so far, even if Tolstoy doesn't seem to like these "sidekicks" very much. But they're thoughtful, steadfast, unpretentious... there's a lot to love, admire, root for, and learn from. SHOSHANA AKABAS

Natasha's star continues to rise. Her idea of quartering soldiers for the evening. Her idea to replace the Kiev plates and Saxony dishes and, gulp, even the count's books, with wounded soldiers in one of those slow, realistic getaways, out of Moscow. MIKE PALINDROME

> Natasha is the one able to put idea into action, but the idea comes from the housekeeper Mavra (credit where credit is due): *"'So. None of your people left in Moscow?' Mavra was saying. 'You'd be better off in somebody's house... This one, for instance. The masters are all moving out.'"* ANSER

"The admiration of others was that grease for the wheels which was necessary if her machine was to run perfectly freely."
   I want Natasha to be perfect, but she isn't, as Tolstoy occasionally reminds us. BOB HILLMAN

"The countess was accustomed to this tone... and being accustomed to it, she considered it her duty always to fight against whatever was expressed

in that timid tone."
    The sign of a long marriage: pushing back based on the tone of the voice alone. **LAURA SPENCE-ASH**

Delighted by Rostov's pride in Natasha's passion, generosity for the wounded, even if he's pointing out his wife's been schooled. She's not the only one Natasha's outpaced. I love how Tolstoy has Rostov refer to his children as *"eggs"* instead of chicks. **ROSEANNE CARRARA**

Instead of further hoarding the wealth created by the serfs packing it, the Rostov family experiences a raising of consciousness: "Reduce your own suffering by striving to improve the lot of the majority" (Peter Lavrov). **SIGRID PAUEN**

"One of my eyes was afflicted, but now I've got both eyes open." "The count had a sty."
    The magical absurdity of war and rhetoric, later chased down by Joseph Heller. An unexpected thrill to read it here. **ANNIE LIONTAS**

Pierre's benefactor pronounces some of the hardest words: *"War is the most difficult submission of a human being's freedom to God's laws."*
    War is where selfless people overcome fear of death. The most senseless violence points to something true. **THOMAS J. KITSON**

What are five artifacts that stay with you from *War and Peace*. For me: Napoleon's white glove, dust, the young French soldier's stirrup with his foot caught, the handkerchief tied around the prince's jaw, the cook's shirt tucked up before she is hit by a missile. **ANNIE LIONTAS**

Spurs, the Rostov house band, Anisya's rye cakes and honey, juniper strewn for death, Black Madonna. **MISS MAINWARING**

The charcuterie-type board at Uncle's (I want sparkling mead!), Natasha's lilac-colored dress, Prince Bolkonsky's bed behind the piano, Hélène's bosom at the opera, Andrei's oak tree. **BLAIR EMSICK**

THE COMFORT OF OBJECTS

"But Natasha did not give in, threw all the things out, and quickly be-gan repacking, deciding that the inferior domestic carpets and extra dishes should not be taken at all."

For reasons I can't quite pin down, I feel incredibly worried about the costly Persian carpets in these pages, and that the family find a way to bring them. I worry, as I read it, about the impossible loss of their objects as they are fleeing Moscow, and I'm not sure why I don't feel a parallel concern for the dying soldiers. I'm not sure if it's my own limitations and keen awareness of the cost of antiques, or something in how Tolstoy has written it so that the soldiers feel vague and fictional, while the furnishings feel like they really exist—that if the family were able to pack them and bring them that something irretrievable would not be lost.

They could come back and re-set up their lives.

It's strange to me that it's the carpets that I hang my hat on here. It's also not clear for whom, if any of the characters, I have sympathy. Natasha turns out to be an expert at packing and problem-solving, and then she heroically unpacks everything to transport the soldiers, but she also feels really chaotic to me. Sonya, who does track the objects, doesn't seem to do so because of their beauty or fear of loss or attachment, but more out of a diligent sense of record-keeping. And Berg, who shares my interest in antiques and sniffing out a bargain, well, he's truly terrible. SARA MAJKA

DAY 61
MAY 17

START
Volume III,
Part Three, XVII
"Towards two
o'clock the
Rostovs' four
carriages"

END
Volume III,
Part Three, XXI
"the troops
were now
moving
forward."

YIYUN LI

Andrei in the caleche, Pierre in the crowd, Natasha in the carriage: it's one of the few scenes in which they are together in the novel, but never have they carried a conversation among themselves. What one would not give to see the three of them sit down and talk.

—

He himself was carried away by the tone of magnanimity he intended to employ in Moscow.

Napoleon imagining what he will do to Moscow is like Boris envisioning how to spend Julie's money before he proposes.

—

Moscow was empty.... It was empty as a dying-out, queenless beehive is empty.

A dedicated beekeeper, Tolstoy makes a non-beekeeper feel desolate, as he makes a reader two hundred years later feel for the abandoned city.

THE VIEW OF MOSCOW

Which scenes, as of now, are most vivid for you? For me: Natasha at her uncle's, Andrei listening out his window, Pierre and the comet, and Napoleon losing his mind. ILANN M. MAAZEL

> Not most vivid but amusing and leaving a lasting impression: the awkwardness and embarrassment shown by Bagration at the banquet held to honor him. The war hero *"not knowing what to do with his hands."* ANNE RUNNING SOVIK

> Nikolai looking up at the clouds! ALI FRICK

> The sleigh ride under the stars, also when all the soldiers tried to show off their river-crossing talents near Napoleon, and they drowned while he was looking the other way. JENNIFER

> Someone watching something: Nikolai watching the old wolf emerge from the thickets, or Alpatych watching people set fire to the barn in Smolensk, or six-year-old Malasha watching the council of war from her seat on the stove. ROBERT BUTLER

I woke up this morning thinking I could look out the window and see Moscow. I can't recall such an experience with a novel before. Being *in* its world so thoroughly. MURRAY SILVERSTEIN

Almost felt pity for Napoleon as he paces before Moscow, imagining himself bestowing benevolence upon the conquered city, while *"awaiting what to his mind was a necessary, though external, observance of propriety—a deputation."* Bendito. ZULMA ORTIZ-FUENTES

A shopkeeper *"blathering"* as Moscow is looted: *"Why weep for your hair when your head's cut off."* Good question. MURRAY SILVERSTEIN

The view of Moscow, *"cupolas glittering like stars in the sunlight,"* followed by the beehive rumination, made me wonder: what's the indefinable quality that makes a city beautiful, exciting? My own city is so humbled, so quiet, a shell. I am here, but I miss it. WAYNE SCOTT

DAY 62
MAY 18

YIYUN LI

START
Volume III,
Part Three, XXII
"The city itself,
meanwhile, was
empty"

Mishka playing the clavichord with one finger and the yard porter seeing himself for the first time in the mirror—even if they don't survive the fire of Moscow, they have encountered the essence of life: art and self-reflection.

END
Volume III,
Part Three, XXV
"began shouting
and dispersing
the clustering
carts."

—

See what they've done to Russia! See what they've done to me!

How easily catastrophes are taken personally.

—

Kutuzov, frowning, glum, was sitting on a bench by the bridge and playing in the sand with his whip, when a caleche noisily galloped up to him.... The commander in chief of Moscow, the proud Count Rastopchin, took a whip in his hand, went to the bridge, and began shouting and dispersing the clustering carts.

Rastopchin is never more stupid than when he's next to a man thinking with a whip in the sand.

WRATH

"As often happens with hot-tempered people, wrath had already taken hold of him, but he was still seeking an object for it." ANTHONY DOMESTICO

Rastopchin tossing a victim, like a piece of meat, to appease the ravenous mob. And the mob, overcome by an excited fury and *"feverish haste."* After today's reading, I need to do something uplifting, and get those 1812 Moscow scenes out of my head. ZULMA ORTIZ-FUENTES

So sickened by today's reading, I'm going out to work in the garden. I'll be back when I stop hating Rastopchin, who Tolstoy keeps telling me is not really to blame. MISS MAINWARING

Moscow abandoned and no leader willing to stand up and say why. And Rastopchin weasels out of any culpability for a man beaten to death. PATRICIA CLARK

Rastopchin and Vereshchagin might be what Tolstoy had in mind in writing that those at the top of the hierarchy are the least free. Only later does Rastopchin realize that he could have acted otherwise. Tolstoy wants to explain him, not excuse him (I think?). MIKE LEVINE

Tolstoy's muse Homer taught us similes (like bees). JOHN NEELEMAN

> Hungry as wolves that rend and bolt raw flesh,
> hearts filled with battle-frenzy that never dies—
> off on the cliffs, ripping apart some big antlered stag
> they gorge on the kill till all their jaws drip red with blood.
> HOMER (THE ILIAD)

DAY 63
MAY 19

YIYUN LI

START
Volume III,
Part Three, XXVI
"Towards four
o'clock in the
afternoon"

END
Volume III,
Part Three, XXIX
"lay down on the
sofa and fell asleep
at once."

In the kitchens they made fires and, with their sleeves rolled up, baked, kneaded, and cooked, frightened, amused, and fondled the women and children.

All those domestic verbs preceding *"frightened"* and then, that most frightening *"fondled."*

> What a string of verbs, made all the more ominous by those rolled-up sleeves. LAURA SPENCE-ASH

—

Pierre imagines assassinating Napoleon while the drunkard Makar Alexeich points the pistol to a servant, calling him Bonaparte: great minds think alike.

—

There was nothing terrible about a small, distant fire in a huge city.

Tolstoy has these one-sentence paragraphs like tightly coiled springs. They are nearly missable in a thousand-page novel, and perhaps for that reason one always feels one has to read even more closely, for fear of missing a sharp-edged diamond in a majestic landscape.

CHARACTER PREVAILS

War and Peace is full of memorable vignettes; My Dinner with Ramballe is among my favorites. Depressed meets joie de vivre. Earnestness meets sleazy. A modern-day Truffaut or Malle needs to do a film adaptation. **SALVADOR ORTEGA**

Sympathetic toward Pierre, up to today—near insanity, because he is forced to eat what a servant eats, vodka instead of fine wine, lumpy sofa, can't change his underpants. These are reasons to dislike camping, not to lose touch with reality and plan an assassination. **BRIAN OLSON**

Pierre morbidly fantasizes about murdering Napoleon (War), then before we know it he's drinking buddies with a French officer and they're toasting Natasha (Peace). **SARAH MEYER**

Poor Pierre. Character prevails. Faced with the charming, oblivious, garrulous, comical, and entertaining Captain Ramballe, he can't help reverting from *"close to insanity"* back to his normal self. **MICHAEL G. FAULKNER**

"Le Fond c'est l'amour." The generous self-evaluation of the superiority of French culture. Kvass: *"limonade de cochon!"* Say no more. **SIGRID PAUEN**

Y'all are so hard on Ramballe. He's a Frenchman! Dines better with a dinner companion. Is handsome. Knows how to make love to a woman. Not husband sex (Pierre, Hélène). Or juvenile fantasizing (Pierre, Natasha). I'm captivated. **MISS MAINWARING**

The Ramballe effect! Pierre begins the chapter thinking the only thing that matters is killing Napoleon and ends the chapter thinking the only thing that matters is loving Natasha. **ROBERT BUTLER**

Today Tolstoy articulates what it means to be Russian thus: *"that vague, exclusively Russian feeling of disdain for everything conventional, artificial, human, for everything that most people consider the highest good."* **ELLIOTT HOLT**

DAY 64
MAY 20

START
Volume III,
Part Three, XXX
"The glow of
the first fire"

END
Volume III,
Part Three, XXXIV
"Pierre was placed
separately under
strict guard."

YIYUN LI

"Who is there to put it out?" came the voice of Danilo Teretyich... and he suddenly gave an old man's sob.

Many weep at the fire. Some tears are more painful to read. This is the proud Danilo who, at the hunt, raised his whip against the incapable Count Rostov.

Many must be weeping at the burning of Moscow. Tolstoy wants us to see the proud serf—feisty and unruly half a book ago—sob.

—

Natasha standing at the open window, listening to the adjutant's moaning and imagining Andrei wounded: an echo of their first meeting, with Andrei listening to her voice through the open window and imagining her happiness.

—

The smoke became thicker and thicker, and it even became warm from the flames of the fire.

The fatal winter sneaks into the novel: Sonya chilled, Natasha's feet cold, the French officer looting for boots, the fire making the air not hot but merely warm.

WE ARE ALL MORTAL

Oh, Pierre! Finally—Resolute! Determined! Active! I am so proud of you. A marked difference here from Natasha's sudden spring to noble action. She is acting on her own behalf. He is acting without regard for himself. **SARA BETH WEST**

So many echoes of these scenes in the literature that follows *War and Peace*. I was reminded so powerfully of this gorgeous passage from Tennessee Williams about what we must rescue from the burning building:

> The world is violent and mercurial—it will have its way with you. We are saved only by love—love for each other and the love that we pour into the art we feel compelled to share: being a parent; being a writer; being a painter; being a friend. We live in a perpetually burning building, and what we must save from it, all the time, is love. **WAYNE SCOTT**

Pierre the hero! His goodness finally unleashed; indecision not conquered but weaponized as a strength. (Abandoning the assassination attempt to rescue Muscovites might be the first time that, after losing heart for a Plan A, he's actually changed course.) **OLIVIA WOLFGANG-SMITH**

Pierre finally stopped thinking so hard for once and RAN INTO A FIRE??? TO RESCUE A CHILD???ANDREI AND NATASHA REUNITED??? Tolstoy is giving us too much I am now so scared he's just gonna take it all away again. **EMMA KIESLING**

As Napoleon sleeps those misled by Rastopchin suffer, while the elite has fled and watches from afar. **SIGRID PAUEN**

The pages with Pierre wandering through a burning, conquered Moscow are high lit, bringing the war to the peace. I adored the exchanges between Pierre and the French marauder who rescue the child together: *"Goodby, Fatty. We must be human, we are all mortal you know!"* **MATT GALLAGHER**

VOLUME
FOUR

YIYUN LI

START
Volume IV,
Part One, I
"In Petersburg,
in the highest
circles,
a complex
struggle"

END
Volume IV,
Part One, V
"kissing her
plump little
hand."

There is some talk about a war, Anna Pavlovna has a soiree. The Battle of Three Emperors has been lost, Anna Pavlovna has a soiree. Moscow is burning, Anna Pavlovna has a soiree. Anna Pavlovna's soirees, a refrain of the novel, are as consistent and life-sustaining as the seasons and stars—as indestructible as nature.

—

The lovely countess's illness came from the inconvenience of marrying two husbands at once.

Hélène's downfall is summarized in an understatement as flawless and hilarious as her clever stupidity.

She feels like the most modern character in the novel: as contemporary as a celebrity whose raison d'être is to live up to her status in the eyes of the public. Hélène's true tragedy is that she offers little for us to ponder over; even the most imaginative reader could not find a reason to spend much time thinking about her.

—

Princess Marya and her late father, whom Mrs. Malvintsev evidently did not like, and... Prince Andrei, who evidently was also not in her good graces.

A glimpse of Marya's mother through the aunt. Family antipathy is fertile ground for the imagination.

WHAT'S LEFT OUT

There's solace in the troubles of 1812: slut shaming, friend-zoned bffs, posturing advisers, conniving gossip, and waves of misinformation as a capital city empties. JANSON

Tolstoy has such a range of tones: so chilling in showing how society relishes (not) naming what kills Hélène, and then so warm in his critique of Nikolai's egotism: *"it had never occurred to him that the pastime which he found so amusing might not be so for someone else."* MOLLY ELIZABETH PORTER

> I love how Tolstoy not only writes of what his characters experience, but what they don't, and can't. JULIA AZAR RUBIN

As Yiyun Li pointed out re: dreams, I'm struck by the scarcity of flashback and backstory in Tolstoy's method. After a thousand-plus pages we haven't been told what happened to Andrei's or Anatole's mothers or to Dolokhov's father, right? MARK RAY LEWIS

> Or why Andrei married Lise, or how Andrei and Pierre became friends... I've read an article that looked at drafts of *War and Peace* to show how Tolstoy deliberately removed backstory, maybe to create a sense of immediacy, mystery, or not be weighed down by exposition. MOLLY ELIZABETH PORTER

> Pierre has not been provided with a backstory because he himself doesn't seem to refer to such. His is the capacity to live in the present. His challenge had always been to find his place and fill it with his presence (manifested by an awkward physicality). ELOPE_

> Pierre is a blank screen for the reader to project upon. He has no personality. BRIAN OLSON

DAY 66
MAY 22

YIYUN LI

Mlle Bourienne... looked at Princess Marya with bewildered astonishment. A skillful coquette herself, she could not have maneuvered better on meeting a man she wanted to please.

One has to admire Mlle Bourienne for remaining consistently herself: romance is the only narrative that matters for her, the lens through which she makes sense of the world, of men and women. Even a war cannot shift her from that position, not even half an inch.

—

That gaze expressed entreaty, and fear of refusal, and shame at having to ask, and a readiness for implacable hatred in case of refusal.

This sentence summarizes many human relationships. Implacable hatred is not often caused by what is done to one person by another, but by the length of trouble that person takes, the amount of emotion they experience, to make sure that the other person can do nothing.

—

Sonya's whole calculation of telling Natasha about Andrei and writing Nikolai to release him is as exhilarating as her cross-dressing that wins Nikolai's heart: unexpected and satisfying.

A PATTERN OF CIRCUMSTANCES

I am loving this volume for The Women. Maman Rostov's gaze expressing *"fear of refusal, and shame for having to ask."* Marya is only happy when squashing her own dreams. Natasha is Natasha. Sonya ping-pongs between tenderness and agitation... Everyone's FINE! GENEVIEVE WOLLENBECKER

How skillfully Tolstoy has us rooting for both contenders for Nikolai's heart: the sorrowful Princess Marya in one moment, and then the sweet self-sacrificing Sonya in the next. SUJATHA FERNANDES

"She felt with joy the return of that mood of self-sacrifice in which she loved and was accustomed to live, and with tears in her eyes and a joyful awareness of performing a magnanimous act, she wrote..."

I would *never* have written the letter Sonya did, freeing Nikolai, under pressure from the family that raised and supported her as their own. What does that say about me? A kind of litmus test of loyalty, selflessness, prioritizing one's happiness. MIKE PALINDROME

I don't like Sonya. MISS MAINWARING

Really? I feel for her—through no fault of her own she's been put at the mercy of this family that sees her as a burden... I feel for Marya too, which is what makes this love triangle so heartbreaking. SIEL JU

"The Countess let no occasion slip of making humiliating or cruel allusions to Sonya." The countess, like every mother, cares for and looks after the interests of her own children. Poor Sonya, with no mother of her own to fight for her. CLAIRE ADAM

Her sad position has made her wily and jealous. No matter her background, there is no justification for ugly behavior! No excuses. MISS MAINWARING

I was thinking she's like Mlle Bourienne, just trying to make it through life by taking advantage of what is available to her. ZULMA ORTIZ-FUENTES

YIYUN LI

START
Volume IV,
Part One, XI
"From Prince
Shcherbatov's
house, the
prisoners"

END
Volume IV,
Part One, XIII
"the value or
the meaning
of a word or
act taken
separately."

The execution chapter: I often feel I have to read it in one breath, or else I would be seeking a million distractions to avoid finishing it.

P.S. On December 22, 1849, Dostoevsky was led before the firing squad but received a last-minute reprieve.

—

He sang songs not as singers do who know they are being listened to, but as birds do, apparently because it was necessary for him to utter those sounds.

How enviable. I only sing when no one is listening and it is absolutely unnecessary to utter any sound.

—

Pierre sensed that, despite all his gentle tenderness towards him... Karataev would not have been upset for a moment to be parted from him.

Karataev is a balm after the terrible execution chapter... for now.

THE BEST CHARACTER

What an odd thing, to be 1,150 pages into a book and come across the best character inside of it. *"They're the horses' saints. We mustn't forget the poor dumb creatures."* Platon kicks ass. RICK PAULAS

Platon cooks, cobbles. He has a dog. He's upbeat, industrious, doesn't talk till cocktail hour. I've waited a thousand pages for this guy. MISS MAINWARING

Pierre is the perfect person to cook for. Give him lard stew: *"more delicious than any food he had ever tasted."* Give him baked potato: *"he had never tasted anything so delicious."* ROBERT BUTLER

Platon Karataev, who gives Pierre deliciously simple potatoes and is the *"embodiment of everything Russian,"* is a perfect example of Tolstoy's obsession with extolling the virtues of the common man. ELLIOTT HOLT

"Don't grieve little friend." At the core of the novel, Karataev, the embodiment of mere life: clothing, food, shelter and animal companionship. No attachments but a gentle disposition toward all life. SIGRID PAUEN

After the horrific executions, Pierre meets Platon. A sweet reminder: how stories bring us back to ourselves; the stuff of healing. WAYNE SCOTT

The final prisoner adjusting the knot of his blindfold made me think of Tim O'Brien's *Going After Cacciato,* when the prisoner is about to be hung and is very composed, and then a fly lands on his nose, distracting him. TATJANA SOLI

> This is the bit that James Wood says, in *How Fiction Works,* that Orwell cribbed for his famous scene in "A Hanging"—the convict being taken to his hanging steps aside to avoid a puddle. AMITAVA KUMAR

> We are always in our bodies, even at the very end. WAYNE SCOTT

The execution scene made me think of Goya's *The Third of May, 1808.* And the series Disasters of War, which he worked on during Napoleon's war in Spain, particularly *And there is no help* (Y no hai remedio). MODUPE LABODE

DAY 68
MAY 24

START
Volume IV,
Part One, XIV
"On receiving
from Nikolai
the news"

END
Volume IV,
Part One, XVI
"solemn
mystery
of death that
had been
accomplished
before them."

YIYUN LI

Light, impetuous, as if merry footsteps were heard at the door.

Natasha's footsteps are the soundtrack of the novel.

—

Making a great effort with himself, he attempted to come back into life and shift to their point of view. "Yes, this must seem pitiful to them!" he thought.

Not everyone understands the privilege of the dying. Andrei not only does but also lets it go for a moment, feeling for Natasha and Marya. One of the most sympathetic Andrei moments.

—

During the last time they themselves felt that they were no longer taking care of him (he was no longer there, he had left them), but of the nearest reminder of him—his body.

This line reads differently after one has sat with the dying and the dead. Sometimes a book is only waiting for us to experience more of life to understand it better.

STUNNED TO TEARS

It was worth reading the whole book for today's pages. I am undone, stunned to tears. MICHAEL G. FAULKNER

Echoes of Natasha, sitting, knitting, in Virginia Woolf: "Mrs. Ramsay—it was part of her perfect goodness—sat there quite simply, in the chair, flicked her needles to and fro, knitted her reddish-brown stocking, cast her shadow on the step. There she sat." LAURA SPENCE-ASH

> I thought this book would be all pompous abstractions, but the characters are physical beings existing in the physical world: that ball of wool falling to the floor, Natasha holding her breath so as to not wake Andrei. CLAIRE ADAM

> And earlier, the way Andrei's shelling is hurriedly reported feels like it also could have influenced Virginia Woolf in *To the Lighthouse*: "A shell exploded. Twenty or thirty young men were blown up in France, among them Andrew Ramsay, whose death, mercifully, was instantaneous." MOLLY ELIZABETH PORTER

Nikolushka is already seven and yet, *"Prince Andrei kissed him and obviously did not know what to say to him. When Nikolushka was taken away..."*
   For me, maybe the saddest moment in the novel. Father-son relationships in *War and Peace* are invariably stunted. JOHN NEELEMAN

These pages are so stunning. Farewell, dear Andrei. I feel I should have loftier thoughts, but I could not shake the idea of *"a squirrel-fur dressing gown"*; how the awfulness of death would be magnified by the touch of such odious quasi-rodents. WAYNE SCOTT

What's the relationship between the submission of Nikolai and Pierre to the force of circumstances (Nikolai's *"eerie"* feeling, Pierre's *"loss of faith"*) and the uneasiness that shows in the faces of those *"just carrying out orders"* at the execution? THOMAS J. KITSON

I loved Tolstoy's change-up when Nikolai starts comparing Marya's and Sonia's *"wealth"* and *"poverty"*—not dowry or estate (as Countess Rostov suspects), but *"spiritual gifts."* **THOMAS J. KITSON**

I have twice sat bedside alone with dying people to last breaths. It was exactly as Tolstoy describes. Exactly. As or maybe more profound than the birth of my children. I am sorry for all who are denied this privilege, especially now. **MISS MAINWARING**

I've witnessed the event as well. Hard to say I recommend it, but watching did ease my fears over my turn coming around. **BRIAN OLSON**

I believe E. Kübler-Ross said it's the hardest job we'll ever have to do; loved ones can help or make it harder. Marya and Natasha helped him die. Didn't protest, make him fight. **MISS MAINWARING**

I have only sat alone with my father-in-law when he was coming to his end. I talked to him not knowing if he could hear me. **BERRY HOAK**

I had a late and wasted friend, Dee, who, when he was dying, told me the sense of hearing is the last to go, even after death. **MIKE LILLICH**

I snuck away from civilization to go camping and was staring into a fire while Moscow was burning. I read aloud the death of Prince Andrei around the campfire, and even the people who don't know *War and Peace* were stunned. **ANNIE LIONTAS**

The strange lightness of being. *War and Peace* enters the otherworldly and beyond words with Andrei's death. I can't verbalize its effect; read it last night, was in my dreams and still reverberates. **SALVADOR ORTEGA**

The saddest part of losing Andrei was that, with all his admirable aspects, he was not able to (as John Cheever noted of privileged Americans) feel much else other than disappointment. **SALVADOR ORTEGA**

And in his soul, instantly,
as if freed of the
restraining weight of
life, that flower of love
opened, eternal, free,
not bound to this life.

VOLUME IV. ONE. XVI.

How thrilling to reach page 1,000 of the Pevear and Volokhonsky translation! "No battle—Tarutino, Borodino, Austerlitz— comes off the way its organizers supposed. That is an essential condition." That is also an essential condition of novels.

ELLIOTT HOLT

Kind of jealous of all the people tweeting about how they've hit page 1,000. I'm reading on a Kindle and I'm at—81 percent.

SIEL JU

YIYUN LI

One of the signs that the Russian army is ready for a battle is the *"curiosity about what was happening in the French army they had so long lost sight of."*

If long-distance love is hard to maintain, one imagines long-distance enemyship is equally unsustainable. True enemyship requires curiosity, fascination, attachment, even obsession; it requires the enemy to be kept in sight and in thought. And yet true enemyship aims for annihilation as consummation. What comes after, then? Casual enemyship? Which, like a casual relationship, must be more frivolous, less inspiring.

—

One of the first bullets killed him, the bullets that followed killed many of his soldiers. And for some time his division went on standing uselessly under fire.

The war has been too long. Even the wordy Tolstoy starts to resort to swift strokes.

—

The battle of Tarutino is like an enigmatic course on a tasting menu: it has a grand name, it arrives at the right time, and it's blatantly bland.

HIS OBSESSION WITH THE GREAT MAN

This may be my favorite volume of *War and Peace*, but it has dry spots—today I kept wanting Tolstoy to get back to intimately observing things like Natasha modulating her breath after picking up her yarn. This passage from Nabokov's *Lectures on Russian Literature* fits my mood:

> What one would like to do, would be to kick the glorified soapbox from under his saddled feet and then lock him up in a stone house on a desert island with gallons of ink and reams of paper—far away from the things, ethical and pedagogical, that diverted his attention... But the thing cannot be done: Tolstoy is homogeneous... Tolstoy was striving, in spite of all the obstacles, to get at the truth. MOLLY ELIZABETH PORTER

"To capture what you love (or don't love) about a book, you have to be attuned to your own interiority—the way a collection of words hits you—and then you give it to others, never sure if these feelings will be shared or slapped away." (Gal Beckerman, *New York Times*) SARA BETH WEST

"What is valuable in Tolstoi, to my mind, is his power of right ethical judgments and his perception of concrete facts; his theorisings are of course worthless. It is the greatest misfortune to the human race that he has so little power of reasoning." (Bertrand Russell) ELEONORE

"This, then, is the great illusion which Tolstoy sets himself to expose: that individuals can, by the use of their own resources, understand and control the course of events. Those who believe this turn out to be dreadfully mistaken." (Isaiah Berlin) JOHN NEELEMAN

> Strange how compulsive, obsessive, repetitive Tolstoy is on this theme. Has any other major writer so belabored a theme in his fiction? He thinks he has refuted Napoleon somehow but his obsession with the *"great man"*—*"genius"*—seems to argue against his own ideas. JOYCE CAROL OATES

YIYUN LI

START
Volume IV,
Part Two, VIII
"Napoleon
enters Moscow
after the
brilliant victory"

END
Volume IV,
Part Two, XII
"Pierre felt
that this view
obliged him."

In the letter to Alexander, Napoleon *"considers it his duty to inform his friend and brother that Rastopchin has arranged things badly in Moscow."*
Chapter after chapter after chapter after chapter on history... and then a wry sentence like that. LOL

—

He ordered his troops to be paid in counterfeit Russian money he had made.

A hilarious sentence to close a hilarious chapter, after Napoleon's endearing words to *"Citizens!"* and *"Craftsmen and labor-loving artisans!"* and *"You peasants."*

—

The French generals lost the sixty-thousand-man Russian army... it was only owing to the skill and, it seems, the genius of Murat that they managed to find, like a pin, this sixty-thousand-man Russian army.

What joy to imagine dour Tolstoy on the day he wrote this.

AZOR, FLOPPY

The way Tolstoy begins each part—moving from macro human affairs to the plight of the individual—is that of a meteor falling to earth, or a leaf.
ANNIE LIONTAS

The shifts in scope are enough to give you vertigo. **OLIVIA WOLFGANG-SMITH**

"We have paid for the right to look the facts simply and squarely in the face, and we are not going to give up that right."
My new motto for life. **MARGARET HARRIS**

"Nothing supplies the truth except the will for it." **SHIRLEY HAZZARD**

Too many variables—the relativity of "good" or "bad" except for outliers, confirmation bias—make history, micro and macro, impossible. **BRIAN OLSON**

The only way I could tolerate the polemic: to imagine Tolstoy as a character, the curmudgeonly uncle who endlessly repeats his gripe (which his listeners ignore). Have I ever been more grateful to see Pierre and the purple dog appear? Is this that moment when, the end so obviously in sight, we focus solely on our beloved's failings to make the parting easier? **WAYNE SCOTT**

Oh, I love the *"long, purplish dog"* that appears outside Pierre's prison shed. With four names—Azor, Femgalka, Gray, Floppy—no breed, *"everything an object of pleasure for it"*... as Moscow smolders... what an astonishing paragraph! **MURRAY SILVERSTEIN**

The dog is blue-gray in my translation but in any case I would really like a puppy like it during this quarantine. **SIEL JU**

Now I know Briggs *is* the best. Our dog Azor/Floppy is lavender-gray.
MISS MAINWARING

All we have left is kindness—knit socks, don't let bright light shine in a dying man's eyes. Share your potato. **BRIAN OLSON**

YIYUN LI

START
Volume IV,
Part Two, XIII
"In the night
of the sixth
to seventh of
October"

END
Volume IV,
Part Two, XIX
"along their
same fatal
path to
Smolensk."

One had to wait and endure.

Patience and time, these are my mighty warriors!

"Wait and endure"; "patience and time." They sound like clichés, but they are life-sustaining words.

—

Red as fire, the glow of the rising full moon spread on the edge of the horizon, and the enormous red ball wavered astonishingly in the grayish haze.

That rising full moon and that grayish haze: a magnificent image. Fast forward to a century later, and Isaac Babel writes, in "Crossing the Zbruch," as though seeing the world again through Tolstoy's eyes, catching majestic nature in wartime:

> The orange sun rolls across the sky like a head
> after a beheading, and a tender light illuminates
> the canyons in the clouds.

—

Shcherbinin lit a tallow candle, causing the cockroaches that were gnawing on it to flee.

Just as he hears the cricket on the night of Natasha's dramatic reunion with Andrei, Tolstoy sees the cockroaches as tens of thousands of people's fates turn. It reminds me of C. S. Lewis's reminiscence of World War I, when he is shelled by Germans:

> I think it was that day I noticed how a greater
> terror overcomes a less: a mouse that I met (and a
> poor shivering mouse it was, as I was a poor shiv-
> ering man) made no attempt to run from me.

ALL THIS IS IN ME

"Pierre looked into the sky... 'all this is mine, and all this is in me, and all this is me!'" Pierre, like Andrei, learns from the sky. It reminds me strongly of *Siddhartha* by Hesse, Buddha, and Elie Wiesel's *Night.* KRISTIN BOLDON

And Whitman. ZULMA ORTIZ-FUENTES

Pierre internalizes the sky and the whole world in a way Andrei could not—he activates the microcosm/macrocosm, whereas Andrei couldn't enter the whole without dying into it. THOMAS J. KITSON

"His letters to Mme de Staël." Five of the letters she wrote to him were actually addressed to his wife, Princess Kutuzov, who Turgenev called an old monkey! SIGRID PAUEN

It was said "there are three great powers struggling against Napoleon for the soul of Europe: England, Russia, and Madame de Staël." (Madame de Chastenay) ROBERT DEAM TOBIN

When I run into Madame de Staël, I always think of A. J. Soprano, telling his parents quoting her, "One must choose in life between boredom and suffering." TERESA FINN

Sending a blank piece of paper to your frenemy, what an act of ingenious spite. ANNIE LIONTAS

Moments after I read about Tolstoy's theory of history and the individual role in it, I read about Larry Kramer, fiery activist from another era's pandemic; a counter to Tolstoy's more modest take on a person's ability to effect big change. WAYNE SCOTT

YIYUN LI

START
Volume IV,
Part Three, I
"The battle
of Borodino,
with the
subsequent
occupation
of Moscow"

END
Volume IV,
Part Three, VI
"'Well, tell
me about
yourself,'
he said."

Oh the long chapters on war strategy. Tolstoy certainly didn't read someone from fifth century BC, whose name was Sun Tzu and who wrote a more succinct book called *The Art of War*.

—

Petya, abashed by Denisov's cold tone and supposing that the cause of it was the state of his trousers, was straightening them under his greatcoat.

Tolstoy understands that, of all the pressures in war, for a boy like Petya the state of his trousers is the most unbearable one.

—

This wound, which Tikhon treated only with vodka, internally and externally...

Yet another memorable character named Tikhon. *"Internally and externally"* seems physiologically and psychologically sound.

READERS

My sister reminds me that *War and Peace* isn't meant to be read as a modern realist novel. **ELLIOTT HOLT**

> Tolstoy himself called this book an epic, not a novel. In his eyes, his first real experiment with the European novel was *Anna Karenina*. **KATHARINE HOLT**

> Any great work of art is larger than its creator. Tolstoy was helping create the genre's future without realizing it. Not unlike Kutuzov, who led best doing nothing. **MISS MAINWARING**

> Every text becomes itself, in spite of an author's intentions! But I also think that *War and Peace* reads like a hybrid of an epic and a realist novel. **ELLIOTT HOLT**

> The count knew what he was up to, meditating on history as the ancients did on fate—but his means, his tools, are those of Western realism. Tools quite beautifully handled, no question. **JOHN DOMINI**

> I don't know if we can take Tolstoy at his word, but it's interesting to think about generic expectations! **KATHARINE HOLT**

> But it does read like a Russian *Iliad*. **ELLIOTT HOLT**

While Tolstoy is a wonderful psychologist and his characters ring true centuries later, he rates much lower as a quantifier-scientist. He would have flunked high-school physics. And his use of *always* when theorizing invites skepticism. **SALVADOR ORTEGA**

A first version of *War and Peace*, only partly published (three-tenths) during Tolstoy's lifetime, contains much less of war strategy, and a much different ending! **TORBJÖRN WINGÅRDH**

YIYUN LI

START
Volume IV,
Part Three, VII
"Petya, having
left his family
on their
departure from
Moscow"

END
Volume IV,
Part Three, XII
"joyful and
calming thoughts,
memories, and
images that
came to him."

It seemed to him all the time that he was not where what was most real and heroic was now happening. And he hurried to get where he was not.

Petya rushing to death: one of the most devastating and pointless races on horseback.

—

Petya falling asleep against his wish; the French drummer boy dropping off because he is hungry and cold and frightened. If only they could be like Sleeping Beauty and wake up in a better time.

—

There is no situation in the world in which a man can be happy and perfectly free, so there is no situation in which he can be perfectly unhappy and unfree.

The perfectly unhappy could be a subject for a novel: literature tends to be crowded with the imperfectly unhappy.

HE CLOSED HIS EYES

Petya's death is one scene I remember from my first reading of *War and Peace*, forty years ago. I was nineteen, not much older than Petya, and in the service. I remember watching a hurricane from the flying bridge of a ship at sea, and never thinking I could die. LAWRENCE COATES

My son is so angry about state of the US I'm worried for his safety. He is Petya and Denisov. I am Kutuzov.... Feels like there is not one cell of my life unaffected by this book. MISS MAINWARING

"He began to recall whether he had done any other stupid things."
My new favorite line, poor Petya. BRIAN OLSON

Dying in battle after the war has been essentially determined—like Paul Bäumer in *All Quiet on the Western Front* and Inman in *Cold Mountain*. Petya's quick, banal death carries a particular futility to it, even in a story of many pointless combat deaths. MATT GALLAGHER

Petya is very Last Supper, here is my body eat of it, here are my raisins, here is my coffeepot drink of it. Food, generosity in literature are so pure, we feel an unnameable but impending loss. ANNIE LIONTAS

"He closed his eyes. And on all sides, as if from far away, sounds trembled, began to harmonize, scattered, merged."
Tolstoy gives the souls of his characters a kind of reprieve-home before death. Andrei: love for his enemy. Petya: exaltation. STACY MATTINGLY

So Dolokhov saves Pierre's life. That's irony on many levels. Dolokhov, so cold and cruel, yet sympathetic in a complex way. Tolstoy seems to be saying that in war, you need a Dolokhov. Denisov, griping about rain, etc., Petya, and Andrei, are less useful. JOHN NEELEMAN

> Brash, reckless, graceful under pressure but not one for moralizing over potential war crimes? Dolokhov would have made a helluva Navy SEAL had he been born in another time and place.
> MATT GALLAGHER

DAY 74
MAY 30

START
Volume IV,
Part Three, XIII
"At noon on the
twenty-second,
Pierre"

END
Volume IV,
Part Three, XIX
"to threaten,
but not to lash
the running
animal on
the head."

YIYUN LI

Cocking its hind leg and hopping on three, to prove its agility and satisfaction, then dashing along again on all four, barking at the crows that sat on the carrion. Gray was sleeker and merrier than in Moscow.

Sleeker, such a complex word: it makes one feel happy and cringe at the same time.

—

Karataev looked at Pierre with his kind, round eyes, now veiled with tears.

Dolokhov's *"gaze flashed with a cruel gleam."*

The eyes of the soon to be executed and the eyes of the executor are equally unsettling.

—

They all went, not knowing themselves where they were going or why. The genius Napoleon knew still less than others, since no one gave him orders.

The inconvenience of being a genius: being loster than all the other lost souls; being lostest, really.

HE WAS AFRAID OF HIS PITY FOR THIS MAN

I'm struggling to understand Pierre's actions, thoughts, feelings around Platon's execution. Will you share your ideas? MISS MAINWARING

Maybe: If you stare death in the face for too long, it threatens to break you. HEATHER WOLF

Pierre is aspirational. In the progression from esthetic to ethical to religious, he for the most part is in the ethical. Karataev has reached the religious level, which both attracts Pierre yet makes him uncomfortable, especially when Karataev is suffering. SALVADOR ORTEGA

It's a fitful bit of the novel, Tolstoy forgetting momentarily that he is a novelist, not a sermonizer, and Pierre doesn't know what to do with himself in such a vaguely constructed scene. WAYNE SCOTT

I think I disagree! Great scene. Pierre is in an altered state of consciousness. Similar to that of Nikolai after he is unhorsed near the novel's beginning (when he throws his pistol at the approaching Frenchman and runs). JOHN OTROMPKE

"He was afraid of his pity for this man." Pierre is simply trying to survive physically and spiritually. ZULMA ORTIZ-FUENTES

A retreat to the head to hide from the heart. ANNE RUNNING SOVIK

Unwilling to accept the pain of what is happening, he tries to avoid it by pretending it isn't happening. ELLEN MASON

I think the story of the innocent suffering merchant that Platon told the night before was his way of saying goodbye, to Pierre and to the world. He could go no farther. Pierre got this, at some level, and so was ready to let him go. MURRAY SILVERSTEIN

I thought Platon was killed because he decided he could go no farther—he sat down and refused to move. In the context of the story he told the previous night, his death was in fact a salvation. BROADBEAN

As I move toward *War and Peace*'s final pages, it's hard not to feel that Tolstoy's project of viewing humanity as a never-ending project cannot have a happy, novelistic conclusion. The characters will go on. So will the novelist. When I turn the last page... what will Pierre's next grandiose mistake be? What will happen to the doctor who kissed Andrei on the lips? We know the trees will continue growing, that the sky will be gray, then turbulent, then blue. ADRIENNE CELT

Something I admire about Tolstoy: he sure gives his characters room to grow. If they're plain, they become beautiful—arrogant, humble. Cavalier, bound to duty. It's like he's saying to us readers, Look, you don't always have to be this way. ANNIE LIONTAS

"The aim of an artist is not to solve a problem irrefutably, but to make people love life in all its countless, inexhaustible manifestations. If I were told that I could write a novel whereby I might irrefutably establish what seemed to me the correct point of view on all social problems, I would not even devote two hours to such a novel; but if I were told that what I should write would be read in about twenty years' time by those who are now children and that they would laugh and cry over it and love life, I would devote all my own life and all my energies to it." LEO TOLSTOY (1865)

Tolstoy has certainly helped me to better "love life in all its countless, inexhaustible manifestations" in *War and Peace*. But I'm not entirely convinced he wouldn't also love to "solve a problem irrefutably." Such a complicated man. MOLLY ELIZABETH PORTER

THE MOST MEMORABLE SEGMENT

Yesterday, on May 29, 2020, as you read volume 4, part 3, chapters 7–12, my son, George, was born. I'd like to thank all of you and A Public Space for giving me a lot to do, think about, and talk about while I worried about my wife and child in the age of Covid.

I can't imagine that volume 4, part 3 is anyone's favorite chunk of *War and Peace*: it's cold and grim, but it will probably be the most memorable segment as I read it during quiet moments of her labor. Petya's mad dash, the liberation of Pierre, Tolstoy's argument that historians write histories *"of the beautiful words and sentiments of various generals"* seems extra gripping, even as I had a lot on my mind. And particularly Tolstoy's and Pierre's sympathy (however misguided) for Platon's crazy optimism.

Thanks to Yiyun Li for giving us so much to think about. I'm planning to print out the entire web page and put it in a binder to keep in my book collection. A very memorable spring of reading—I'll be forever grateful.
ANDY BLACK

DAY 75
MAY 31

YIYUN LI

START
Volume IV,
Part Four, I
"When a man
sees a dying
animal"

END
Volume IV,
Part Four, V
"a lackey has
his own idea
of greatness."

She saw his face, heard his voice, and repeated his words and the words she had said to him, and sometimes she invented new words for herself and for him.

If one character from the novel is capable of inventing new words after a death, it has to be Natasha.

—

"Neither the sun nor death can be looked at steadily": La Rochefoucauld's words ring true, and these chapters after Andrei's death and Petya's death hurt one's mental retina.

—

For a lackey there can be no great man, because a lackey has his own idea of greatness.

Kutuzov is the *"old man in disgrace."* Napoleon is the *"grand homme."* For every historical figure in the novel, there is a lackey plaiting slippers out of cloth trimmings.

A WOUND IN THE SOUL

"Only together were they not offended or pained."
Natasha and Marya, grieving the loss of Andrei together. The comfort found in collective grief, something so many have not been able to do in recent months. LAURA SPENCE-ASH

Have read a decent amount of war lit in my years. I've never encountered a scene that so acutely captures the shock and raw despair of a family learning their son has died in battle as Tolstoy does with the Rostovs regarding Petya. One page of wrenching brilliance. MATT GALLAGHER

Natasha *"concentrating all the power of her love to somehow take onto herself the surplus of sorrow crushing her"* might exemplify best the жалость "pity" Russians associate so closely with love: wishing you could save them from suffering. THOMAS J. KITSON

The amount of emotional labor done by the women in this book is astounding. It's a full-time job. SIEL JU

"And now it will never be possible to put it right."
Mourning, trying to save oneself *"from reality in a world of insanity"* is shown to be a uniquely personal experience. (Pierre. Natasha. Countess. Marya.) SIGRID PAUEN

Tolstoy understands grief. A spiritual wound that might heal or might even kill you, and this *"wound in the soul, like a physical wound, can be healed only by the force of life pushing up from inside."*
And that force of life is love. MICHAEL G. FAULKNER

A meditation on different kinds of grief. Denisov howls when confronted with Petya's death. Dolokhov seems indifferent (but I don't think is). Pierre turns his back on Platon, buries grief in order to go on, while a dog howls. ZULMA ORTIZ-FUENTES

The ancients debated what life was better—a long boring life where the dull years pile up, or a potentially short one but full of risk, thrills, chills. Dolokhov has opted for the wild, and he saw Petya's dream, took him behind enemy lines. BRIAN OLSON

This opens Dolokhov up a bit more—he knows he's leading Petya into danger, but also recognizes he's making Petya's dream come true—just as long as Petya manages his recklessness. Dolokhov is ruthless enough to make sure he does. Denisov is softer, can't rein it in. THOMAS J. KITSON

In my next reading, I'm going to pay closer attention to the Dolokhov sections. I dismissed him as the bad guy too easily. He did try to dissuade Anatole from Natasha debacle. ZULMA ORTIZ-FUENTES

Dolokhov deserves his own spinoff novel. He has no conscience (reminds me of Patricia Highsmith's Tom Ripley). An asset in a warrior, card shark, or in basketball a shooting guard. SALVADOR ORTEGA

He deeply loves and cares for his elderly mother and disabled sister. I wouldn't say no morals. (Courage is a virtue too.) STEPHEN COULON

That's why he fits the antihero category. He's not a villain. "Unconscious" hoops players have no qualms about taking the last shot in a game. If you have no conscience, there's less to fear. James Cagney's character in *White Heat* loved mom too. SALVADOR ORTEGA

Tolstoy's depiction of the insanity of grief astonishes. WAYNE SCOTT

History repeats. During unrest, the ruling class will attempt to preserve a system that allows them to continue profiting off of people who are hurting and oppressed, under the guise of keeping the peace. **KATY EINERSON**

Tolstoy's earlier point proves true: History has constants. And human behavior is unchangeable. **DEREK SHERMAN**

"The Russians, half of whom died, did all that could be done and were not to be blamed because other Russians sitting home in warm rooms proposed they should do the impossible."

These words feel right, heavy on the day after I show up and watch my city burn. **ANNIE LIONTAS**

I survived my childhood, a gothic horror, by reading. Reading was hope; confirmation; escape. The day I read *The Sound and the Fury,* I knew it was my world that was crazy, not me. Today I can't read. I cannot pick up the book. **MISS MAINWARING**

It is confusing right now. Reading and commenting about a book (even this book) can feel... self-indulgent? Likewise, in deep grief I couldn't read fiction. It seemed absurd. And yet if I'd read today's pages, they'd have given succor. **MICHAEL G. FAULKNER**

"Thoughts and words which serve to express them are not what move people."

When does Tolstoy abandon novel writing? Immediately after this book? **BRIAN OLSON**

DAY 76
JUNE 1

START
Volume IV,
Part Four, VI
"The fifth of
November was
the first day"

END
Volume IV,
Part Four, XI
"And so he died."

YIYUN LI

It was impossible to take bread and clothing from hungry and much-needed soldiers in order to give it to the not harmful, not hated, not guilty, but simply unneeded French.

Indifference kills.

—

Kutuzov did not understand the significance of Europe... For the representative of the national war there was nothing left but death. And so he died.

"And so he died." The death of one of the most memorable characters, delivered in one astonishing line.

MIKHAIL IU. LERMONTOV

Alone, I come out on to the road. The stony way glistens through the

    mist; the night is still, the wilderness is listening to God, and star is

    talking to star.

All is solemn and wonderful in the sky; the earth is sleeping in a pale

    blue radiance... Why then do I feel so much pain and heaviness of

    heart? Am I waiting for something, regretting anything?

I expect nothing more from life, and do not regret the past at all. I

    seek for freedom and peace, I would like to find oblivion and to

    fall asleep...

But not with the cold sleep of the grave: I would like to fall asleep

    forever so that the forces of life would slumber in my breast, and

    that it would heave in gentle breathing;

so that an enchanting voice, delighting my ear, would sing to me of

    love day and night, and a dark evergreen oak would bend and

    rustle over me.

PROSE TRANSLATION FROM THE RUSSIAN BY DIMITRI OBOLENSKY

The end of chapter nine leans on this poem by one of Tolstoy's favorite poets (and it has Andrei's oak in the last line). Thomas J. Kitson

DAY 77
JUNE 2

START
Volume IV,
Part Four, XII
"Pierre, as
most often
happens, felt
the whole
burden"

END
Volume IV,
Part Four, XVI
"'It's the first
time she's
spoken of him
like that.'"

YIYUN LI

The legitimate peculiarity of each person.

This seemingly simple discovery of Pierre's is why we can easily recall not only the major characters but also the most minor and fleeting characters from the novel. And the dogs and hares and horses.

—

"Yes, he's a very, very kind man, when he's under the influence, not of bad people, but of such people as I," the princess said to herself.

The confidence people put in that capital *I*. It serves as just the right megaphone for the ego that sees no limit to its amplification.

—

The face, with its attentive eyes, with difficulty, with effort, like a rusty door opening—smiled.

One of the most memorable Natasha moments: the first smile after her beloved's death.

TRANSCENDENCE

Nearsighted Pierre has always been trying to see what's in the distance; now he can comfortably lose not just the telescope, but maybe even the glasses Hélène hated so much, and has, in his freedom, more to stare at than his own bare feet. THOMAS J. KITSON

Some posit grace is granted and not earned; even then, Pierre's sudden transition to the religious stage of being feels, well, fictional. At the same time, more than any *War and Peace* character, Pierre seeks transcendence, which is the best thing about him. SALVADOR ORTEGA

Having experienced it in my own life—newfound well-being and content- ment—I know it isn't fictional. I also know it is predicated on one's physical and material well-being, which Pierre and I share. I suspect his road will get rocky again. MISS MAINWARING

So Pierre continues to drift from fad to fashion, seeking something to sustain him, intellectually and morally, while remaining so passive and uninvested that nothing can possibly stick for long. He is an eye without a mind or a heart. M. C. RUSH

He is kind. BERRY HOAK

Is he, though? Or is it just that with his utter lack of ambition, he just can't be arsed to do anything distressful to anyone? M. C. RUSH

"General Buonaparte has of late found much amusement in the improve- ment of the garden at Longwood and in the cultivation of plants and shrubs." HENRY BATHURST (JUNE 2, 1820)

Tolstoy in his conceived circles of hell has Napoleon by himself at the deepest, with Germans where it's not quite so hot, and doctors somewhere between the two. Had good reasons for this, given medicine's state of the art at the time. SALVADOR ORTEGA

DAY 78
JUNE 3

START
Volume IV,
Part Four, XVII
"Pierre was
taken to the
big, well-lit
dining room"

END
Volume IV,
Part Four, XX
"'Right, Marie?
It has to be so...'"

YIYUN LI

Marya Abramovna... told me everything that has happened to me or should have happened. Stepan Stepanych also taught me how to tell my story. Generally, I've noticed that being an interesting person is very convenient (I'm an interesting person now); people invite me and tell me about myself.

I always go back to these words of Pierre's when I have a complaint about life. He is gentle and kind, what right do I have to be impatient? One wants to live up to his standard.

—

That same mischievous smile, as if forgotten, remained on her face for a long time.

Natasha's smile is like her singing: there is only a pause, never a full stop.

—

I must do everything to make it so that she and I are man and wife.

What joy to see Pierre finally make one statement without self-doubt, guilt, uncertainty, philosophical or theological discourse.

HE JUST LOVED THEM

He did not wait to discover *"good qualities in people before loving them,"* he just loved them. What an amazing thing to carry around in your pocket, Pierre. ANNIE LIONTAS

"She caught the unfinished word in its flight and took it straight into her open heart, divining the secret meaning of all Pierre's mental travail." Just beautiful, Natasha. ALIX CHRISTIE

"The servants came with sad and stern faces to change the candles, but no one noticed them" and *"But he had no sooner entered the room than he sensed her presence with his whole being, by the instant loss of his freedom."*

What is the relationship between paying attention to someone—the quality of deep attention, love—and captivity—to be imprisoned, to be captivated, to be loyal to the dead, to be held hostage by a guest? WAYNE SCOTT

When did the "marriage plot" happy ending turn corny? BRIAN OLSON

Into the clever versus real woman brawl: I apply what a novelist says to what they show. Clever is Anna Pavlovna, Julie Karagin, Sonya, Hélène. Real is Marya, Natasha, Anisya, Marya Dmitrievna. I personally choose group B. MISS MAINWARING

I think Sonya is real. Have we heard the last from her? MIKE LILLICH

Ah, you men. You love Sonya. I don't trust her! MISS MAINWARING

Praise be that Natasha is a "real" woman, not merely an "intelligent" one! M. C. RUSH

Lost heart for commenting lately, but kept up with my reading. From today's pages: *"To go on with the previous conversation is impossible; to talk about trifles is shameful, and to be silent is unpleasant, because... silence is like a pretense."* OLIVIA WOLFGANG-SMITH

EPILOGUE

DAY 79
JUNE 4

START
Epilogue,
Part One, I
"Seven years
had passed
since 1812."

END
Epilogue,
Part One, V
"that gloomy
state of mind
which alone
enabled him
to endure his
situation."

YIYUN LI

After a long march, we are entering the epilogue-land. I have scribbled "yes" many times in the margin, and as many times "huh?" All the same it's never boring to imagine a conversation with Tolstoy.

—

If we allow that human life can be governed by reason, the possibility of life is annihilated.

Another possibility: In an alternative universe where life, governed by reason and logic, gives everything such a pristine order, people would long for illogic, unreason, chaos. For the residents of that universe, this world would be their fantasy.

—

Not only is he great, but his ancestors, his brothers, his stepsons, his brothers-in-law are great.

To occupy an immortal place in history as Napoleon's stepson or brother-in-law? Thank you but no.

LINGER WITH ME

To start with, a quotation from David Bromwich's *A Skeptical Music*: "Any critic who quotes vividly has done half the job one wants to see done." It's through quotation, Bromwich explains, that we see "evidence of taste and touch"—not the taste and touch of the critic but the taste and touch of the writer she's considering. Or, rather, we see the critic's taste and touch in her ability to reveal the writer's taste and touch. To read well is to recognize those moments when the writer is at her most characteristic and alive. Look here, the critic says. Linger with me.

Another quotation, this one from the poet Katie Ford: "I make my bed every morning / I don't know where to start / so I start with the bed. / Then I fall to my knees against it."

All spring, I'd wake every morning and not know where to start. Teaching was remote. The future was unsettled. So I'd begin with Tolstoy: reading slowly, looking for a favorite quotation, then tweeting it out.

> MAY 11: *"Suddenly something happened; the little officer said 'Ah' and, curling up, sat on the ground like a bird shot down in flight."*

> MAY 18: *"As often happens with hot-tempered people, wrath had already taken hold of him, but he was still seeking an object for it."*

Finding that perfect sentence briefly brought the day back to its moorings. Time felt disciplined again.

R. P. Blackmur described poetry as language that "adds to the stock of available reality." This period saw that stock drastically limited. What a relief to still have Tolstoy, the realist of realists. I couldn't go to a dull party but I heard what one sounded like: *"There was nothing bad or inappropriate in what they said, everything was witty and might have been funny; but that something which constitutes the salt of merriment was not only missing, but they did not even know it existed."*

I didn't see real-life strangers but I saw their fictional counterparts: *"The coachman's eyes lit up at the sight of the wine. He declined out of propriety, then drank and wiped his mouth with a red silk handkerchief tucked inside his hat."*

As reality begins to open back up. I can hear Platon whispering, *"Lay me down like a stone, raise me up like a loaf."* ANTHONY DOMESTICO

DAY 80

JUNE 5

START
Epilogue,
Part One, VI
"At the beginning
of winter,
Princess Marya
came to
Moscow."

END
Epilogue,
Part One, IX
"which she
involuntarily
remembered
at that
moment."

Nikolai's making *"it a rule to read all the books he bought"* reminds me of a friend who makes a rule never to comment on a book she hasn't read—an essential element of democracy, though in reality people often rush to convictions before knowing and understanding.

—

Like a cat, she became accustomed not to the people, but to the house.

The saddest truth about Sonya: when people she's attached to fail her, she reattaches herself to a place and a position.

—

He thought of how she would be when he, as an old man, started taking her out, and would do the mazurka with her, as his late father used to dance the Daniel Cooper with his daughter.

From a quick-tempered hussar to a family man, Nikolai's progress speaks of something I want to believe: Characters do change, so do people. And I want to believe I am comforted by that change.

A QUIET SADNESS

If anything about the plot of this book were determined beforehand, it may be this marriage: Tolstoy's parents were Count Nikolai Ilyich Tolstoy and Princess Marya Nikolaevna Volkonskaya. MOLLY ELIZABETH PORTER

I've had a hard time warming to Nikolai throughout, and then this note that he *"made it a rule to read all the books he bought."* Who could love a man like that? KATHRYN PRITCHETT

I'm conflicted about Nikolai. But I admire how he overcomes his family's lassitude and dissipation to be a good worker, an economically responsible man, and—perhaps—a reasonably good father. JEFFREY MORRIS

"Once he'd begun managing the estate out of necessity, he soon took such a shine to farming that it became his favorite and almost his exclusive occupation."
  Nikolai at the height of Tolstoyan blessedness: happy doing the thing he has to do. (All I remembered of him from last time was his *"dark mood"* after his father's death, and that wasn't fair to him at all.) THOMAS J. KITSON

I was curious about the Laocoon signet ring that Nikolai breaks while beating his serfs. Winckelmann described the Vatican statue of Laocoon as "noble simplicity and quiet grandeur." ROBERT DEAM TOBIN

Looking for evidence of Marya as Tolstoy's ideal (regarding faith), I notice that only those who drew near to her are left alive and "happy" at the end. SARA BETH WEST

Tolstoy gives with one hand, takes away with other. Marya is happy, but with *"a quiet sadness."* She realizes *"there was another happiness, unattainable in this life, which she involuntarily remembered at that moment."* No absolutes in *War and Peace*. ZULMA ORTIZ-FUENTES

The great math Tolstoy does in *War and Peace* is to hand the character every variable but one, thereby making happiness impossible—for how desperately do we suffer for the little that remains unattainable. That ache is what reminds us we're human. ANNIE LIONTAS

DAY 81
JUNE 6

YIYUN LI

START
Epilogue,
Part One, X
"Natasha was
married in the
early spring
of 1813"

END
Epilogue,
Part One, XIII
"when the
stockings
were finished."

Denisov... looked at Natasha with surprise and sadness, as at an unfaithful portrait of a once-loved person.

Like many people, poor Denisov doesn't see that Natasha has no responsibility to make her life make sense to others, but only to herself.

—

I, for one, want to applaud Natasha as a wife and a mother: she's consistently herself, caring only about what matters to her (not society but her family), and doing things with all her might (including nursing her own children, *"an unheard-of thing"*).

—

He wanted to be learned and intelligent and kind, like Pierre.

Andrei should be happy that his son, brought up by Marya, has such a discerning mind.

AN HONEST TELLING

To Tolstoy, liberty is a dangerous aspiration. A serf is offered his freedom, and declines, expressing contentment. Tolstoy dramatizes the serfdom of all women, without judgment, intrusive as he is in the novel. Pierre, now not free, is finally content. JOHN NEELEMAN

What do we think about the domestication of Natasha? The last time I read *War and Peace* I was hopping mad at Tolstoy. I have more sympathy for epilogue Natasha now. MARGARET HARRIS

I've not felt the age divide among Tolstoy Together as much as I do now. The epilogue for me is an honest telling of married life, how women and men mature and find meaning together even as they fail at times. I lost my "spark" years ago. A damn relief, I can tell you. MISS MAINWARING

> A reader once complained to Dorothy L. Sayers that her character Lord Peter Wimsey had lost his "elfin charm" in her later books. She replied "Any man of forty-five with elfin charm ought to be put in a lethal chamber." MARGARET HARRIS

But I might challenge Tolstoy on his notion that a breastfeeding mother can overfeed a baby, which was impossible in my experience. MISS MAINWARING

Natasha is still like Hélène. She is a body in which the soul is only visible on occasion. THOMAS J. KITSON

I love that Natasha gains substance and presence (even if within the confines of marriage and motherhood). *"She was neither sweet nor amiable"* and does everything contrary to the rules of how a society wife should behave. And she's happy. ZULMA ORTIZ-FUENTES

"The boy, who was only beginning to suspect about love, put together the notion that his father had loved Natasha and had bequeathed her, upon dying, to his friend."
    Children create a story of the unknown past in order to explain the present. LAURA SPENCE-ASH

YIYUN LI

START
Epilogue,
Part One, XIV
"Soon after
that, the
children
came to say
good night."

END
Epilogue,
Part One, XVI
"'I'll do
something
that even
he would be
pleased with...'"

She felt a submissive, tender love for this man, who would never understand all that she understood.

Oh, happy marriages: Marya's love for Nikolai has an echo in Vera's attitude toward Berg.

—

One thing confused her. It was the fact that he was her husband.

Natasha is the rare character who doesn't feel shy about acknowledging her confusions, especially the irrational ones.

—

Nikolenka felt weak from love: he felt strengthless, boneless, and liquid.

What a sentence about the love that happens only at an impressionable young age. Love in adulthood strives for a distinctive shape.

MINOR CHARACTERS

Of the *War and Peace* characters whose ultimate fates don't make it into the epilogue, which one do you most want to hear about and why is it Dolokhov? A partial list of others:

1. Vera and Berg
2. Boris and Julie and
   Anna Mikhailovna
3. Ippolit Kuragin
4. Captain Ramballe
5. Tushin
6. Tikhon
7. Bilibin
8. Marya Dmitrievna
9. Anna Pavlovna
10. Uncle
11. The mysterious
    Rostov cousin
12. The lavender-gray dog

MARGARET HARRIS

All of the minor characters to whom Yiyun has drawn our attention. I'd love to read their stories. MINOR READER

Oh Marya Dmitrievna, the terrible dragon—what happened to her? ANSER

"Vassilisa, a village headman's wife, who destroyed hundreds of the French." What I would give for a chapter about this female-led partisan detachment! SIMONA SARAFINOVSKA

(And what did her husband think?) WAYNE SCOTT

I wanted to see Uncle *"Right you are!"* again. But no. The memory of the evening spent with him remains a distant guiding star for Natasha and her brother. And us. MURRAY SILVERSTEIN

Reading *War and Peace* and thinking about its length has me thinking that I, with good health, probably only have about a hundred more books left in me and probably a thousand more books I want to read. M. C. MALTEMPO

DAY 83
JUNE 8

YIYUN LI

START
Epilogue,
Part Two, I
"The subject
of history is
the life of
peoples and
of mankind."

END
Epilogue,
Part Two, IV
"we will get
the history of
monarchs and
writers, and
not the history
of the life of
peoples."

Epilogue, Part Two: every time I get here, I have a moment of déjà vu of being in the army, nodding off when the instructor of Marxist Philosophical Theory analyzed a Hegel paragraph, then, waking up, realizing we were still in the same paragraph.

Still, every time I make a point of reading every word in the second part of the epilogue, the smart and the baffling and the repetitive. I'm not embarrassed to say that this feels like a mental tug-of-war with Tolstoy. I won't feel at peace if I give in.

THEN, LISTEN

Finally done with all his characters, Tolstoy becomes the Deep Thinker, struggling to give birth to a Theory of Everything. Nutty, but still, the unmoved mover moves me. MURRAY SILVERSTEIN

Theorizing (again) about history. I wish that I'd read part two before part one—they are the wrong way round! I feel like I ate my last slice of cake and then had to take my medicine. MICHAEL G. FAULKNER

I'm not doing well with you guys criticizing my man Tolstoy. I know you're cranky and all, but I'm sticking with him to the end. He's infinitely better than my first two husbands and most men I know. MISS MAINWARING

I'll focus on the positive for a while! ROBERT DEAM TOBIN

Thank you! MISS MAINWARING

Might be a bit of a mansplainer though. LAWRENCE COATES

"I love *War and Peace* for the wonderful, penetrating and true descriptions of war and of people but I have never believed in the great Count's thinking.... I learned from him to distrust my own Thinking with a capital T." ERNEST HEMINGWAY

"*Then, listen:*
   '*Louis XIV was a very proud and conceited man...*'"
   I really hope your translations made you feel you were reading a bedtime story for little children. THOMAS J. KITSON

It's the only part of the epilogue I've liked so far, precisely because he stripped it all down to such basic ideas. AURELIA DRAKE

The condescension is so thick in the Russian text, he even follows it up with: "*You'd be wrong to think this is mockery, a caricature of historical descriptions.*" THOMAS J. KITSON

YIYUN LI

START
Epilogue,
Part Two, V
"The life of
peoples
cannot be
contained"

We are nearly there. I have a fantasy that we all turn into the spoon player at the beginning: "*A spoon player, despite the weight of his ammunition, nimbly leaped out in front and walked backwards.*"

So much to look back at. So much to play on our spoons.

END
Epilogue,
Part Two, VIII
"from their
plastering point
of view,
everything
comes out flat
and smooth."

—

Clive James said he could finish *War and Peace* in one breath if there were a long enough breath. I could imagine a long breath lasting until the last fifty pages, when I do feel I need several breaths.

IN OTHER WORDS

Do you mean I just spent eighty-five days and read over a thousand pages to have a happy ending that true love is the answer for redemption of the world. MILLIE

"In other words," Tolstoy has written fifteen hundred pages of *War and Peace* to arrive at *"power is a word the meaning of which we do not know."* ANNIE LIONTAS

Briggs is: In a word, power is power. Or something like that. I'm in the process of erasing this epilogue from my short-term memory. MIKE PALINDROME

Just finished *War and Peace*. Turns out, it's a 1,140-page argument against putting Great Men on pedestals. ROBERT BUTLER

What about great women on icons? MISS MAINWARING

You know how, very occasionally in your life, there's a "before and after" reading experience? Well reading *War and Peace* with Tolstoy Together has been that for me—a milestone not just in reading but in living, and I'm not even exaggerating... I'm altered. MICHAEL LANGAN

Experiencing this book over such a stretch is like decanting it; it begins to breathe, to take on new color and flavor, and to perfume everything with its own essence. ALEXANDRA SCHWARTZ (THE NEW YORKER)

"The chief thing that made him ready to weep was a sudden, vivid sense of the fearful contrast between something infinitely great and illimitable existing in him, and something limited and material, which himself was, and even she was."
What is your favorite sentence in all of *War and Peace*? DAVIS THOMPSON

One day left. Still holding out hope Denisov and Sonya will fall in love and move into an apartment at Bald Hills. Unless Vera and Berg claim the apartment as her dowry. I'm sure the old count died owing Berg money. JANICE AXELROD

DAY 85
JUNE 10

START
Epilogue,
Part Two, IX
"For the solution
of the question
of freedom and
necessity"

END
Epilogue,
Part Two, XII
"it is just as
necessary to
renounce a
nonexistent
freedom and
recognize a
dependence
we do not feel."

Dear Friends,

We've done it!
Like the bees, we have
foraged and shared, built
together and supported
one another. The world is
far from friendly to bees
and flowers, but may we
go onward and upward,
without fatigue, without
impatience.

Gratefully yours,

YIYUN

SO WE'VE COME TO THE END

This book has been a solace and an energizer. I find it *so* directly relatable to our lives today. Sigh. Upheaval. History. Influence. Freedom. Dependence. The Human Condition. I will miss the book and this community.
LYNNE MORROW

> It has helped us, my wife and I, elders, weather this storm. I read and each day on our walks, she says, "So what happened today."
> MURRAY SILVERSTEIN

Did I read *War and Peace* out of free will, or out of inevitability? We did it, Mum. YVONNE YEVAN YU

Mostly I read to escape. Reading *War and Peace* with Tolstoy Together was the opposite—running toward something. I'm a better person because of this book and experience. I can still read big books and have big thoughts. Strangers are kind. MISS MAINWARING

I've learned now to not be intimidated by a tome. As Shakespeare said, "Perseverance, dear my Lord, keeps honour bright." I never liked routine, but Tolstoy Together has changed my view. Thank you, everyone. HARRY JOHNSON

So we've come to the end. I'm very grateful for this collective experience—it will stay with me. You've held my hand from afar. MICHAEL G. FAULKNER

"Life, as he looked at it, had no meaning as a separate life. It had meaning only as a part of the whole, which he constantly sensed." I've sensed this so much while reading in this community. MOLLY ELIZABETH PORTER

At first, I kept up with the reading but traveled alone with my carriage shades drawn. When I threw them open here you all were, each one alone and all of us together. Thank you for the company. DANAI PALEOGIANNI

1,200+ pages, 361 chapters, 100s of characters, 17 parts, 4 volumes, 85 days, 1 glorious masterpiece. Thank you Tolstoy Together for the ride to nineteenth-century Russia. From the soirees to the battlefields, we made it. "Everything I know, I know because of love." JAYDON FARAO

ACKNOWLEDGMENTS

Thank you to everyone who was a part of Tolstoy Together. To the independent booksellers, and to Elliott Stevens. To the mighty team at A Public Space for their efforts and dedication, including Sarah Blakley-Cartwright, Caroline Casey, Miguel Coronado, Megan Cummins, Claire Dauge-Roth, James Li, Anne McPeak, Taylor Michael, Cristina Rodriguez, Kyle Francis Williams, and Deb Wood. To the friends who travel with A Public Space in solidarity through every new adventure, including Katherine Bell, Charles Buice, Elizabeth Gaffney, Mark Hage, John Haskell, Mary-Beth Hughes, Brett Fletcher Lauer, Dapeng Li, Ayana Mathis, Kristen Mitchell, Robert Sullivan, Suzanne Sullivan, Natasha Randall, and Antoine Wilson. To Yiyun Li, for her extraordinary generosity and talent. And to all our fellow readers.

CONTRIBUTORS

FARAH ABDESSAMAD is a French-born, New York–based essayist.

CLAIRE ADAM is the author of *Golden Child* (Hogarth).

SHOSHANA AKABAS is a writer, teacher, translator, and the executive director of a nonprofit that helps refugees resettle in New York City.

ANSER lives in New York City.

JANICE AXELROD is based in Newton, Massachusetts.

JOSHUA BARONE is the assistant performing arts editor and classical music critic on the *New York Times*'s culture desk.

ANDREW BERTAINA lives, teaches, and writes in Washington, DC.

ANDY BLACK is an associate professor at Murray State University.

SARAH BLAKLEY-CARTWRIGHT is a writer and an associate editor at A Public Space.

KRISTIN BOLDON is a writer living in Minneapolis.

BROADBEAN is a keen reader and a civil servant in the United Kingdom.

KIMBERLY BURNS is a partner at Broadside PR.

MATT BURNS is a high-school teacher.

ROBERT BUTLER is a journalist and critic with a PhD in geography.

TIM BYRNE is a bookseller at Avenue Bookstore.

ROSEANNE CARRARA is the author of *A Newer Wilderness* (Insomniac). She lives in Toronto.

ADRIENNE CELT is the author of *Invitation to a Bonfire* (Bloomsbury) and the forthcoming novel *End of the World House* (Simon and Schuster).

RYAN CHAPMAN is the author of *Riots I Have Known* (Simon & Schuster).

EILEEN CHENG-YIN CHOW is associate professor of the practice in the Department of Asian and Middle Eastern Studies at Duke University and co-director of Duke Story Lab.

DAN CHIASSON is the author, most recently, of *The Math Campers* (Knopf).

ALIX CHRISTIE is the author of *Gutenberg's Apprentice* (Harper).

PATRICIA CLARK is the author of *Self-Portrait with a Million Dollars* (Terrapin).

PHILIP F. CLARK is the author of *The Carnival of Affection* (Sibling Rivalry).

LAWRENCE COATES is the author of *Camp Olvido* (Miami University Press).

PHYLLIS COHEN is the founder of Berkeley Books of Paris.

KATE CORDES is a librarian.

STEPHEN COULON is a reader, writer, and public school teacher.

MEGAN CUMMINS is the author of *If the Body Allows It* (Nebraska) and the managing editor at A Public Space.

PIA DESHPANDE is a data journalist and social science researcher.

ANTHONY DOMESTICO is an associate professor of literature at Purchase College, SUNY, and the books columnist for *Commonweal*.

JOHN DOMINI's latest book is a memoir, *The Archeology of a Good Ragù: Discovering Naples, My Father, and Myself* (Guernica).

AURELIA DRAKE is a freelance editor and translator. She is based in Canada.

ROBERT P. DROUIN is a retired dentist living in Ontario.

TOM DRURY is the author, most recently, of *Pacific* (Grove).

MICHELLE EINDHOVEN is a librarian and information professional.

KATY EINERSON is an arts administrator and community gardener.

ELEONORE is based in London.

ELOPE_ is based in London.

BLAIR EMSICK is based in Omaha, Nebraska.

PAMELA ERENS is the author of *Middlemarch and the Imperfect Life,* which is forthcoming from Ig Publishing.

JAYDON FARAO is working toward a PhD in Health Innovation at the University of Cape Town.

DEWAINE FARRIA is a US Marine veteran and the author of the novel *Revolutions of All Colors* (Syracuse University).

MICHAEL G. FAULKNER is based in the Upper Calder Valley in northern England.

DENY FEAR is based in in Victoria, British Columbia. He writes about classical music at *Music for Several Instruments*.

SUJATHA FERNANDES is the author of, most recently, *The Cuban Hustle* (Duke University).

TERESA FINN is a retired English teacher.

STEPHANIE "ABBI" FLETCHER is a special-education high-school English teacher.

ALI FRICK is a civil rights attorney living in New York.

NICK FULLER GOOGINS is a writer and teacher.

MATT GALLAGHER is a US Army veteran and the author of, most recently, *Empire City* (Atria).

KELLY GARDINER is the author of *The Firewatcher Chronicles* (Scholastic).

KEVIN GEORGAS is the co-pastor of Jubilee Baptist Church.

JORIE GRAHAM is the author of, most recently, *Runaway* (Ecco).

JEFFERY GLEAVES is the digital engagement and content senior director at the Academy of American Poets.

LAUREN GOLDENBERG is deputy director at the Dorothy and Lewis B. Cullman Center for Scholars and Writers at the New York Public Library.

RICHARD L. GORELICK is a freelance writer and former restaurant critic for the *Baltimore Sun*.

ANDRÉE GREENE is a writer and educator in Brooklyn.

GARTH GREENWELL is the author, most recently, of *Cleanness* (FSG).

ERIK M. GREGERSEN is a senior editor at *Encyclopaedia Britannica*.

HARISH is a scientist living in Germany.

MARGARET HARRIS is an American-British science journalist.

BOB HILLMAN is a singer/songwriter based in San Francisco.

BERRY HOAK taught in London and Greece and was a guide at Colonial Williamsburg.

RON HOGAN's most recent book is *Our Endless and Proper Work: Starting (and Sticking to) Your Writing Practice* (Belt).

PAULINE HOLDSWORTH is a producer at CBC Radio.

ELLIOTT HOLT is the author of the novel *You Are One of Them* (Penguin).

KATHARINE HOLT is an instructor of history and literature.

HARRY JOHNSON is a retired actor and writer living in Venice, California.

SIEL JU is athe author of *Cake Time* (Red Hen).

MICHAEL KELLEHER is the director of the Windham-Campbell Prizes at Yale University and the author of *Visible Instruments* (Chax).

JOHN KENYON is the executive director of the Iowa City UNESCO City of Literature as well as the director of the Iowa City Book Festival.

FARISA KHALID is a teacher and literary critic and recently completed a PhD in English from George Washington University.

ANSA KHAN is an editor and lives in London.

EMMA KIESLING is currently teaching English in South Korea.

THOMAS J. KITSON's translation of Iliazd's *Rapture* (Columbia University) won a special mention from the Read Russia Prize jury.

PHIL KLAY is the author, most recently, of *Missionaries* (Penguin).

AMITAVA KUMAR is the author, most recently, of *Immigrant, Montana* (Vintage).

MODUPE LABODE is a public historian and curator specializing in African American history.

MICHAEL LANGAN is the author of *Shadow Is a Colour as Light* (Lume Books).

MIKE LEVINE is an independent editor in New York City.

MARK RAY LEWIS is a writer and beekeeper.

J. MIKE LILLICH is a writer and editor for the Labor and Employment Relations Association.

ANNIE LIONTAS is the author of the novel *Let Me Explain You* (Scribner).

JON LITTLE is a civil rights lawyer living in Indianapolis.

CATHRINE LØDØEN lives by the sea in Norway and teaches kindergarten.

FIONA MAAZEL is the author, most recently, of *A Little More Human* (Graywolf).

ILANN M. MAAZEL is a pianist, composer, lyricist, civil rights lawyer, and partner at Emery Celli Brinckerhoff Abady Ward & Maazel.

MISS MAINWARING is a former playwright and hellbent old lady.

SARA MAJKA is the author of the story collection *Cities I've Never Lived In* (A Public Space/Graywolf).

M. C. MALTEMPO is a forever aspiring author.

ASH MARTIN is a psychotherapist in New York City and a former assistant editor at A Public Space.

ELLEN MASON is a retired bookkeeper living in Forest Hills, New York.

AYANA MATHIS is the author of *The Twelve Tribes of Hattie* (Knopf).

STACY MATTINGLY launched the Sarajevo Writers' Workshop in Bosnia and Herzegovina in 2012.

PHILIP MCGARRY, OBE is a Fellow of the Royal College of Psychiatrists.

ANNE MCGRATH is a writer living in the Hudson Valley.

DIANE MEHTA is the author of *Forest with Castanets* (Four Way).

SARAH MEYER is a writer living in Santa Monica.

TAYLOR MICHAEL was an A Public Space Editorial Fellow and is an MFA student at Columbia University.

BENJAMIN T. MILLER is based in Durham, North Carolina.

REBECCA MIRSKY is a sustainability consultant and based in Tucson, Arizona.

JEFFREY MORRIS is based in Helena, Montana.

LYNNE MORROW is a music director.

KIRTAN NAUTIYAL is a writer and a practicing hematologist and oncologist.

JOHN NEELEMAN is a lawyer and the author of *Logos* (Homebound).

CATHERINE OATES is the director of Wild Surmise Literary Management.

JOYCE CAROL OATES is the author of numerous books, including most recently, *American Melancholy* (Ecco).

MO OGRODNIK is a writer, director, and professor in the Film Department at New York University's Tisch School of the Arts.

BRIAN OLSON is a retired English instructor.

SALVADOR ORTEGA is a family physician in Salem, Oregon.

ZULMA ORTIZ-FUENTES is a writer and former New York City public school English teacher.

JOHN OTROMPKE writes criticism under his own name and fiction under various pseudonyms.

ANN PACKER is the author of *The Children's Crusade* (Scribner).

DANAI PALEOGIANNI is from Greece and based in Portugal.

MIKE PALINDROME is the president of the Literature Supporters Club and frequent guest on the podcast *History of Literature*.

SIGRID PAUEN is based in Trumansburg, New York.

RICK PAULAS is a writer and reader living in Brooklyn.

CARL PHILLIPS is the author, most recently, of *Pale Colors in a Tall Field* (FSG).

MOLLY ELIZABETH PORTER is a PhD student in English at the University of Washington.

ELLEN PRENTISS CAMPBELL is the author *Frieda's Song* (Apprentice House).

LAURA PRESTON is an associate editor at A Public Space and a coordinator at Harvard University's Carpenter Center for the Visual Arts.

KATHRYN PRITCHETT is a writer living in Oakland, California.

JULIA AZAR RUBIN is a Bay Area–based English teacher and writer with an MFA from Mills College.

M. C. RUSH is a poet and the author of, most recently, *Know All Things To Be Like This* (Cyberwit).

RICHARD Z. SANTOS is the author of *Trust Me* (Arte Público).

SIMONA SARAFINOVSKA is based in Saint Louis, Missouri.

JOSEPH SCAPELLATO is the author of *The Made-Up Man* (FSG).

ALEXANDRA SCHWARTZ is a staff writer at the *New Yorker*.

WAYNE SCOTT is a writer, psychotherapist, and teacher.

JENNIFER SEARS is a writer and English teacher at City Tech in Brooklyn.

PAUL SERVINI, originally from Wales, has taught languages in several countries. He is now retired and is based in Dole, France.

DEREK SHERMAN is the author of *Race Across the Sky* (Plume).

MURRAY SILVERSTEIN is the author of *Master of Leaves* (Sixteen Rivers).

MICHELE SMART is based in Sydney, Australia.

CHARLIE SMITH is a house cleaner and pet sitter living in Frederick, Maryland.

ADAM SNYDER is a reader from Grand Rapids, Michigan.

TATJANA SOLI is the author of *The Removes* (Sarah Chrichton).

ANNE RUNNING SOVIK is a retired copyeditor living in Northfield, Minnesota.

LAURA SPENCE-ASH is a writer and the Founding Editor of *CRAFT*.

SHANNON STONEY is a professor of visual art at Volunteer State Community College.

KENNY SUI-FUNG YIM works as a librarian assistant in Boston, Massachussetts.

ROBERT SULLIVAN is the author, most recently, of *My American Revolution* (FSG) and is a contributing editor to A Public Space.

JILL TATARA is a photo editor and author of picture and middle-grade books.

TATIANA is based in Brazil.

MARK TERCEK is the author of *Nature's Fortune* (Basic).

DAVIS THOMPSON is an English literature teacher at Auburn High School in Auburn, Alabama.

ROBERT DEAM TOBIN is a professor of German and comparative literature at Clark University.

BARBARA VANDENBURGH is the books editor for *USA Today*.

S. KIRK WALSH is the author of *The Elephant of Belfast* (Counterpoint).

ESMÉ WEIJUN WANG is the author of *The Collected Schizophrenias* (Graywolf) and the novel *The Border of Paradise* (Unnamed).

RUBY WANG is a graduate student studying English and American literature at New York University.

SARA BETH WEST is a writer and reviewer living in Tennessee.

LOWELL MICK WHITE is the author of *Normal School* (Buffalo Times).

NICK WHITE is the author of the story collection *Sweet & Low* (Blue Rider).

KYLE FRANCIS WILLIAMS was a 2019 A Public Space Writing Fellow and is an MFA candidate at the Michener Center for Writers at UT Austin.

COLIN WINNETTE's next novel, *So You Think You Can Dance?*, is forthcoming from Soft Skull.

HEATHER WOLF is a writer based in Annapolis, Maryland.

OLIVIA WOLFGANG-SMITH is a writer living in Brooklyn.

GENEVIEVE WOLLENBECKER lives and teaches in Brooklyn and is working on her first novel.

YVONNE YEVAN YU is a writer living in Hong Kong.

CARMEN ZILLES is based in New York City.

ISAAC ZISMAN is a writer from San Francisco.

CREDITS

COPYRIGHT

NOTES

_____

DATE STARTED

_____

DATE FINISHED

DATE: _____

_____

Pages read: _____

_____

_____

_____

_____

_____

_____

_____

_____

_____

_____

_____

_____

_____

_____

_____

_____

_____

_____

_____

_____

_____

_____

_____

DATE:

Pages read:

DATE: _____

_____

Pages read: _____

_____

_____

_____

_____

_____

_____

_____

_____

_____

_____

_____

_____

_____

_____

_____

_____

_____

_____

_____

_____

_____

DATE:

Pages read:

DATE:

Pages read:

DATE:

Pages read:

DATE:

Pages read:

DATE:

Pages read:

DATE:

Pages read:

DATE:

Pages read:

DATE:

Pages read:

DATE:

Pages read:

DATE:

Pages read:

DATE: _____

Pages read: _____

DATE:

Pages read: